the gathering
By: Diane J. Ackerman

ISBN: 978-1-60461-578-4

Printed in the United States of America
Edited by Julie Barnes and Bernie Walsh
Cover design by Eli Blyden of CrunchTimeGraphics.com
Illustrations by Nola Banta and Eli Blyden

Additional copies of this book are available by mail.
Send $15.95 each plus $3.00 S&H to:

Diane Ackerman
315 East Maud Street,
Tavares, Florida 32778

For more information and to contact Diane:

Telephone #: 352-343-3380
E-mail: diane@alternatepathways.com
Web Site: www.alternatepathways.com

Please include your testimony or help received from this book when you write. Your feedback is important to me.

Dedication

I dedicate this book to my Grandchildren, I know I can't change the world, but I can influence my small part of it with all my love *Mema*

Angels

This book is for the … Angels
I pray we won't corrupt
With foolishness and anger
When we're speaking so… abrupt

I implore you … seek your answers
And pay attention too
Then respond with ability
For the mistakes that … belong to you

For when we free our… Angels
To be ALL that they can be
Our world will be a peaceful one
With love… and … harmony

Introduction

This book, it is a Gathering of thoughts and points of view
It's meant to start you thinking … of what is really bothering you
Perhaps you'll want to read it … one time or maybe two
Whatever the case may be it's meant to bring joy to you

The Spiritual Connection

The giraffe, in its spiritual definition, represents one's potential to see beyond the obvious. As the tallest of animals at nearly 18 feet, and with a neck as long as 7 feet, the giraffe may seem clumsy and awkward. However, its weight is distributed quite evenly. It is only vulnerable when it bends down to drink water.

A lesson to gain from this magnificent animal is the ability to view our lives in a way that is both grounded and flexible. And when we choose to grow spiritually, exercising our free will, we will see past the limitations that are set before us. Like the giraffe, we must be willing to stick our necks out and see beyond the obvious.

When we are dealing with deep-seated emotions, we have a tendency to emulate the ostrich, rather than the giraffe. But once we take responsibility for our behavior and forgive ourselves, as well as forgive those who have offended us, we find that we become sure-footed and able to go long distances without a drink, like the giraffe. So the giraffe may serve as a reminder that when we lose sight of what was meant to be (our unconditionally loving God-self) we will sink into a mundane way of life. We risk losing our true Spiritual connection.

Acknowledgements

I will begin by acknowledging and thanking my terrific family for allowing me to be a part of their amazing, dysfunctional world. I suppose I could have taken a bitter point of view, or possibly acquired a whole bunch of guilt from our dysfunctional world. However, I have claimed a different outlook on my life by choosing to see the perfection in it all. I have come to realize that we are truly the writers of our own scripts. This gives us an opportunity to create the beginning, concoct the events in the middle and predict, or what is even more magnificent, choose the characters with whom we want to share the wonders of the future. Throughout this journey, my teachers have presented me with enlightening lessons in patience, understanding, and unconditional love. I have decided to present these truths in poetic form. It is my intention to contribute a lighter side to our darkest fears, and allow my readers to experience their own part in this script we call life.

It is with great gratitude that I applaud all my Teachers, Mentors and Soul-mates, especially the roles played by my father and other family members. And to my children and grandchildren, who are continuing to open my heart and mind to a different way of thinking. I offer a special acknowledgement to Mrs. Rockwell, who taught me to have strength and to forgive and love unconditionally, no matter how hard the lesson. At 59 years of age, I am finally getting it, and *"IT"* was learned by experiencing my own mini-traumas, addictions, and observations.

We often feel that this gift is exclusive to famous spiritual teachers like Gandhi, Dr. Wayne Dyer, Dr. Deepak Chopra, Mother Teresa, Edgar Cayce and countless others who have helped people formulate their personal truths and shape new worlds. From a variety of acquired beliefs and rituals handed down from generation to generation, these subtle inner *knowings* emerge from one's Soul, rising above all doubts to become one with all that is around us.

I thank the doubting Thomases in my life who are closest to me, and through no fault of their own have given me the courage and strength to present this book, not as a lesson but as a journal, looking into the adventure I call life.

Namaste, may the giraffe in your life always be looking over you.

CONTENTS

Preface

Dear Reader,

This book is a collection of "story poems" based on true life experiences of clients, friends and colleagues, addressing the many facets of life's situations, circumstances, dilemmas, joys and solutions. You are not likely to read this book in one sitting. Its intention is to open up and explore the filing cabinets in you minds. If you are one who has a tendency to stay stuck in the "box" of social standards and rules, you may want to approach this book with some caution. Please be advised that this book is not intended to offend or defend any particular belief or dogma. In fact, it is meant to address just the opposite.

This book is intended to open your eyes, to reveal your authentic self. As you read each "story poem," keep in mind that there is no punishment, there is no blame, and there is no guilt. There are only consequences for the behaviors adopted through belief systems handed down to us from past generations and cultures. It is our choice to continue with our addictions to this chaos, or change our paradigms to prescriptions of happiness.

Our lives are a series of stories, and we often tend to hold on to the ones that cause us the most confusion and upheaval. The trend is one of constant wishing for a better ending, rather than committing to a permanent change of perspective, as it is the least destructive course.

Each "story poem" will begin with first impressions, then gradually work its way toward a shift of personal responsibility and change. It is our soul's journey and our sole purpose to learn these chosen lessons, both good and bad, then transcend from the negative outcomes to reach a place of peace and love. The question is: do you want to find a solution, or do you want to stay in the delusions?

Everyone has a drama trauma and a reason for clinging to it, as though it were a down covered crutch. Find the "story poem" that resonates with your particular "story," then read on and take some time to process your thoughts. If you react with a feeling of discord, then I've accomplished my goal of making you think. Use the "story poem" as a tool, and then reexamine the reasoning behind these repeated behaviors. Recognize their role or purpose for feeding the chaos and discomfort that you are experiencing. While some of the stories were taken from students and friends, all of the names have been changed to protect their privacy. You may find that this book will take you several months to process. If a particular "story poem" causes you to question your thought process, do it.

Don't Call Me Stupid!

When I was just a child … I had this book in me
I was told I couldn't write it … I had Dyslexia you see
My teachers called me Stupid … cuz …to them I read real slow
But, I was turning things around that's what they didn't know
So as I got much older my teens I had to be.
I used my sense of humor and made it work for me.
While growing I was lanky and real fast on my feet.
There was no situation … my smart mouth would not meet.
I found myself in trouble for most of what I said.
And before I even knew it … I was in over my head!
I got so much detention I thought I might move in.
Still made my way through High School, although the ice was thin.
The work force was a challenge but, one I did invite!
I found that making money was quite a great delight.
Then one day I realized that *stupid* I was not!
I fed my brain by reading … then gave writing a good shot.
That was when I found the book inside of me
It was sleeping quite so dormant waiting to be freed.
The day I started writing … my soul began to Plea.
Tell the world your troubles and show them you can be.
The same as every other kid who was told she could not read.
It's you that holds the limits that keep you from *SUCCESS!*
By subscribing to the bondage that won't let you express.
So … look into the pockets of your mind and you will see
That in there lies a book, just like the one in Me!
Never! Let another limit you in thought that's the very seed
For which your soul has fought.
Your life is full of choices ... None of which are bad
Just some will make you happy and some will make you sad.
So when you make your choices look through your pride and
see The Consequence, for happiness is setting Ego free.
Of course then you could feed it and so right you would be
But loneliness is part of you … not a part I want for ME!

When I was growing up, one of my mentors was Mrs. Rockwell. She was a neighbor who made extra money to supplement her family income by watching my sister and I after school until my parents got home from work. She had five children of her own, and my sister and I it made seven. Needless to say, after school activities were well planned and on a rather strict schedule. As soon as we got home from school, the routine was to change our clothes, have a snack of Kool-Aid and dough cookies, and then we could go outside to play for at least an hour. And if we didn't have homework, we didn't have to come in until dinner.

I usually had homework because I spent the majority of the time in the classroom trying to figure out the written lessons. The nuns often made me feel stupid, and it seemed as though they would deliberately pick on me to read in front of the class. I dreaded reading; I would often stammer, lose my place and rarely see the words as they were spelt. The Nuns would roll their eyes in disgust and chastise me in front of my peers, making me feel as though I were a real dummy. Math was no picnic either. Unless I had plenty of time to work on a problem, I would inevitably get the wrong answer. I would once again wear my "stupid hat," and while no one came right out and said I was stupid, I certainly felt that way.

Mrs. Rockwell was the epitome of patience. She would have us sit at the dining room table and open our books to whatever we had to complete. These after school classes would last from 3:30 to nearly 5:00. Promptly at 5 o'clock, we would come inside, wash up, set the table, and start helping to get dinner on the table. When Mr. Rockwell came home, we all sat at the table, said the blessing, and then Mrs. Rockwell would put the food on our plates, carefully making sure that we all had an equal portion. Except Mr. Rockwell, who always got a heaping plateful as a nightly reminder that he deserved more, because he worked so hard during the day.

I remember those days with a great deal of love, for we not only ate dinner, we solved the problems of the world. We discussed our day at school, our friends, our enemies, our games, our what nots and our do nots. We always kept in mind the fact that when Mr. Rockwell wanted to speak, he was to have the floor and we were to be quiet. However, with the gentle patience and masterful coaxing Mrs. Rockwell was always able to open the dialogue to allow us to voice our opinions and complete our thoughts. I never felt stupid at the dinner table, even if I was asked to say the blessing. I never felt rushed; I always felt there was time. I was often encouraged to write down my thoughts, especially if I didn't feel comfortable expressing them out loud. I found this to be a great way to vent my feelings. As a young adult, I used my journals to sift through my thoughts, and they became a source comfort and confrontation. This is a practice I highly recommend. In fact, I encourage you to purchase a notebook while you are reading this book. I am sure there will be a few of the story poems that you will relate to, and as you do, please feel free to jot down your feelings. You will be surprised when you read your journal how much you did not understand about yourself. Please be sure to be honest.

"I respect faith, but doubt is what gets you an education"
—Wilson Misner

Journal

I started this small journal as I sat alone one day
I wrote it down on parchment and cried along the way
The truths that I revealed took me in that day
I saw myself, my *Naked Soul*, and put it on display
I knew what was inside me I'd kept so well concealed
I needed to divulge it so I could be well healed
I purchased my behaviors and cried so many tears
For when I faced my true self, it made me face my fears
The things that I'd been hiding in darkest shadows held
The madness I have been feeding was making me so old
My heart it was once healthy and my body too
I pointed all the blame I had at others even you
But, the day I wrote my Journal, it was a *wondrous* day
It freed my heart and soul again. So, I could once more play
The happiness inside me began to grow again
I recognized the faults in me were merely a perception
My need to pay a punishment was really a *deception*
It was just one mans opinion meant nothing more to me
Then the price of a watermelon that value was the *key!*
We put so much importance on things *materially!*
And what was in my journal when repeated rapidly
Meant nothing more than the Melon in its rank of value to me
So as I sat alone that day atonement was my, *Quest*
Though what my Angel taught me …
Was that *at-one-ment* is the *Best!*
To be at one with my *God* as the source who sets me free
I'll enjoy the perfect peace and love … you intended me to be

Over the past fifty plus years, I have observed many different households, starting with my own dysfunctional childhood experience. The difference is that while I am still dealing with a few issues from my own family, I am also sharing my experiences and resolutions with my clients. I have been an anger management coach and workshop facilitator for the past decade. During that time, I have crossed many paths and studied diverse personalities. It is distressing when a client comes into my office feeling completely frustrated. They are frequently confused, often due to their inability to communicate their extreme sensitivities, shattered self esteem issues, and erroneous belief systems passed on by well intending parents, teachers, or preachers.

Throughout my experiences with clients, friends, and family members, and observing it all as a student and a teacher, it has become abundantly clear to me that if we are to have any peace on a personal or collective level, we must each take responsibility for our own personal situations. You can pick up any self help book, go to any self help seminar or spiritual workshop, and the bottom line is always accountability. Many people are expecting the great Guru in the sky to levitate them and bring them above all the worldly ills. The truth is that if we don't accept our part in what we've created for ourselves, then there is no power in the Universe that will change our lives around.

I am a volunteer at a homeless shelter in Central Florida. When dealing with the many guests that go through the system, I am given a different class every four weeks. In the past two years, I have heard an infinite number of excuses for the reasons they have ended up homeless.

The common perception of a homeless person is that of a dirty, drug addicted, irresponsible individual who is living off the system. This is not entirely true or false. The truth is that all those who render themselves homeless create their situations through bad choices. And even when rescued, if not educated, these individuals will most likely end up right back where they started.

Governments all over the world are plagued with hoards of people who are perceived as social misfits for one reason or another. Unless the education starts with the families, we cannot expect our mainstream populous to change. Recent events have proven that this lack of education is not necessarily limited to one particular class in society.

Our family structure has been severely damaged. It doesn't matter how much money a family is making today, because it seems there is never enough time for the children. Most parents are either working so hard to provide the basics, or they are so focused on keeping up with social acceptance that many neglect to spend valuable time with their children, who desperately need a sense of security and belonging. Discipline has become a crime, and genuine affection is perceived as perversion. We may want to reconsider this perception by reexamining our standards. Instead of using judgment and punishment, we should adopt a position of understanding and acceptance. We need to use consequences, rather than punishment, as a measure for discipline.

"If you have made mistakes, even serious ones, there is always another chance for you. What we call failure is not the falling down but the staying down." —Mary Pickford .

I Feel Your Pain

I feel your pain I see your rage … let no man put asunder
It's through this fear and confused haze…
That lives begins to plunder…
Apologies to no avail with society comes disgrace…
Condoning this and condemning that
Our characters are defaced
It's only when we educate that we become so humble
We thought we had the answers …
When our egos began to crumble
The truth is that reality is seldom where we're at …
Our fears have brought these things about …
Only truth will kill that cat!
When hid inside, it's Suicide to think we can resolve
So we substitute with resolute … for a punishment to evolve
We must eradicate these nasty lies … before it is too late
Thus eliminate the mishandling of the things that we all *Hate*
Knowledge and understanding will help to educate
Specifically with a boundary that we can all relate
Then we save our families from the gossip of desire …
Our safety nets are firmly set once we stop …
Singing to the choir

Have you ever wondered why our youth is so attracted to street gangs? Well, possibly because our families don't communicate anymore. Or when they do, it is only to point out what is going wrong, not recognizing what went right. People have a need to belong, either to a family or a pseudo family, and who better to admire than one of your own kind? When a client is unable to communicate because of a feeling of inferiority, low self esteem or stress, they have virtually lost the ability to see a light at the end of the tunnel.

So what do we do to change this mind set? Instead of forecasting disaster whenever people mess up, we might recall a few of our own mistakes, remembering that all too familiar uncomfortable feeling of judgment and ridicule. I doubt that anyone alive has made it through life without making a mistake. People are so willing to pass judgment and point out that "In my day I did this" or "We did it that way" or " Why are you doing it that way?" that they fail to even acknowledge or honor the smallest of achievements.

I don't mean to say that one should ignore constructive advice. I am saying that if you're going to give advice, you must be living it. How can you demand that someone listen to your golden words if you do the opposite of what you are advising? Human nature doesn't work that way, especially when dealing with a headstrong personality. One of the golden rules we so often fail to practice is to LISTEN!

So often we hear the words, but we're not listening between the lines of the pain, confusion, fear or frustration. People often react before thinking, and angry words are exchanged that are not only damaging, but leave scars that last for years. Often these scars are not revealed until our anger is out of control, and we are left alone in a room, wondering how our lives became so empty. It is so easy to pass judgment on people. We need to look behind the closed doors of every mind, for therein lies a candle that magnifies the prisms of a crystal, and when fed with love, will shine brighter than the beacon of a light house. This is the energy we need to focus on, rather than focusing on the petty, mundane gossip that creates chaotic, frenzied behavior, which is fed by hate and jealousy.

"All people want is someone to listen." —*Hugh Elliott*

Crystal

I'm sending you this crystal
And all that it can do
The *energy* that flows through it
Will transmit strength to *you*

Perhaps you won't believe it!
And that's OK with me
I know you have this *energy*
Because… it's what I see

So when you look into this Crystal
With facets … Oh so deep
Recall the *love* around you!
It's in your soul to keep …

Peace

PEACE … started at the table when I was very young
We sat around and shared our day … Of new things we'd begun
None were so important that we felt we could not share
So we sat around and listened to our follies and despair
Soon it spread to Councils of Towns … and Cities too
All were of importance to someone's point of view
Then as we grew larger … *Egos* … came to play
Opinions took a front seat while the families went away
The arguments got louder then violence came to stay
Soon there were no families ... Street gangs would take their place
And if you disagreed you feared … They'd punch your face
They took away your freewill and passed on all their rules
They stole you from your relatives … and made your parents fools
What happened to our families? Perhaps it's time that we return
To re-instill the values our Grandparents who taught us to discern
They were old but they did teach us … to love, honor and obey
Not because we had to ... we wanted it that way
We talked and shared our feelings, played games so we could stay
I miss that big old table … And the pots of chicken soup …
The *Jewish penicillin* that kept away the croup …
Today we watch a TV and the families who are they?
We logged them into history to read about someday
Along with wars of terror and other horrors that came our way
We must revive our families … perhaps change a thing or two
If we don't there'll be destroyed and our kids won't have a clue
So put down all your weapons your side arms and your bombs
Look into your neighbors eyes and see they're … Dad and Moms!
None will see a color, a creed or attitude …
Just good old fashioned sayings … with pleasant platitudes
Now I'm buying me a table to start sitting with my kids
We'll play games and share our laughter …
We'll be a family that *Forgives!*

Listen

I asked you just too … *Listen*
Not formulate your truth
Your ducks inside were quacking
Like trumpets on a Roof!

How dare you give me answers
For that's not what I asked
I merely tried to ventilate
From fears deep in my past

I hope we'll heed this lesson
That we can *both* discern
For God gave us one tongue
And two ears so we could learn!

Perhaps if you stop talking
And look into my eyes
You'll help me find my answers
When I see through my own lies

So show me that you're listening
Please don't criticize
For even if you win you lose
Without some … *Compromise!*

For the past few generations, women have had to join the work force, either to supplement their household income, or because they are the only source of the household income. When I started my family in the late 1960s, my husband was in the Air Force. He was deployed overseas during the Vietnam War. It was necessary that I have a job to survive, so I chose a night job in order to be with my baby during the day. I was blessed by having a family that allowed me to stay in their basement apartment, which also illuminated the need for a day care or babysitter.

When my husband returned stateside, he decided to further his education by going to college. My world was consumed with the household responsibilities and our family, and I realized that I was becoming a single parent, even though I was married. Then my son was born, and my world became one of diapers, bottles, and endless nights of little sleep and constant worries. I wanted life to be perfect, but what I didn't realize was that it already was perfect; after all, I had chosen this reality. I was living during the age when Father Knew Best, Lucy was the dizzy housewife, and Beaver was the little boy always under conviction for a guilty conscience. And then there was the Brady Bunch, the Partridge Family, Fonzie and Richie, Mary Tyler Moore, shows which all portrayed the wholesome family image.

Was life really that way? Hell, no! The 1960s and 70s were years of social turmoil. It was much like today; we lived with an unpopular war, unpopular leader, financial hardships, and a rebellious youth, along with certain parents, teachers, preachers and politicians all sticking their heads in the sand like pompous ostriches. They resorted to hiding from life and laying down rules of how life should be, rather than looking at life the way it was.

Like many young people today, I did not agree with my parents' opinions or philosophies on raising children, nor did I agree with their religious belief systems. So I rebelled. I decided not to force my children to conform to all the rules, just mine. I made many mistakes, but my basic values were strong, and integrity was of utmost importance to me.

Rather than getting angry at my children for lying, I decided to instill in them a sense of integrity, just as my father taught me. Your word is your bond, and this is not a piece of expensive paper, for paper can be torn up or set to flame, but your word is who you are. If you can't be true to yourself, then who can you be true to?

So as not to leave the impression that I was a canonized, saintly figure of a parent, I must clarify a few points. Along with instilling integrity, I was also considered a screamer. If things were not perfect, meeting my standards, I had a bad habit of screaming or using a tone that would instill a sense of fear in my children, which could only compare to the wrath of God. I often wondered why I did so much screaming, after all, it only worked for a while. In time, my children would shut down and pretty much ignore my craziness.

"Children begin by loving their parents; as they grow older they judge them; sometimes they forgive them." —Oscar Wilde

Daughters

I was but a … *Child*
And you were just a babe
I wiped your nose and bottom
And put your cloths away

You came to me for guidance
When things would bother you
But, now that you're a *woman!*
It's ME that bothers you!

It doesn't have to be that way
If *we* would think things through
I'll always be your Mother
But, I can be your best friend too

Now you have a daughter
I watch with great surprise
I see the Love and Conflict
I once saw in your eyes!

I guess it's just a pattern
One we all out grow
Someday you'll want to share with her
The things I let you know

Like put a phone card in your Bra …
And know when it's time to *GO!*

Son

Sometimes you drive me *crazy!*
Because, you move so *slow*
I hate it when you're *lazy!*
I know it's all a … *show!*

Now, I've come to *realize*
It is time to let you *go!*
If you're going to make,
Your *Own* mistakes

I have got to let you g*row!*
Your talented good looking
And such a great delight
You'll make it in this troubled world

Of that I have no *fright*
But, while you're still here with me
I have a simple plea! Turn off that loud music
And give some *"Peace"* to me!

I wanted so much to be my children's closest friend and confident. I lost sight of my original goal and managed to instill the same sense of guilt and fear that my mother and father passed on to me. Eventually, I woke up to recognize that my innate desire to control my entire family and all those around me was going to be the source of my demise, unless I changed. Old habits are hard to break, unless you're really focused on making a change. The old habits become folklore, which eventually grow roots that attach to your soul.

Frequently, young people attach themselves to long term relationships without giving thought to their own aspirations, thinking they need a partner to complete their happiness. What were once perceived as traditions become a source of discomfort. We use little white lies to hide our inner most feelings of frustration. Soon these lies grow and become damaging secrets that are swept under the rug, all just to save face. Young men observe a lack of gender respect for their mothers and sisters through their father's reference to them as being "only a woman." Young women begin to develop an unhealthy feeling of resentment for their male counterparts because of their careless lack of respect.

Or worse yet, these women feel the need to be submissive and subservient due to the examples given by their dominated mothers, who entered into traditionally controlling relationships. These beliefs were passed down from generation to generation by the "normal family" of two parents, where the woman took care of the home and the man worked outside the home to bring home the bacon. Most major decisions were made by both parties, or left to the man of the house because he made the money. This often left the woman of the house feeling somewhat inadequate or incapable of making a decision. It also fostered the male opinion of gender superiority, in spite of the fact that women of the 60's broke many barriers by burning their bras. The caveman mentality is still very much alive, mainly because the human ego (both male *and* female) has an insatiable desire to be right. It is important to replace this belief with one of equality, rather than competition, or this subconscious rivalry will continue to undermine our families.

Ginger wanted it all, the big house, two children, the dog and the SUV. She married the perfect man and created her dream. However, she lost herself in the mix. She confused her material wants with her spiritual needs. Her husband provided her with everything but her self respect. She soon felt trapped and afraid to assert herself. Her doctor medicated her with happy pills, which for years helped mask her discontent. She blamed her anguish on her abusive childhood, all while she was drowning in a sea of repressed anger. Like most people in controlling relationships, she found her true self when she was able to break through her perfect fish bowl life. While to some it may have looked like a self sacrifice, to her it was utter emaciation.

"No one can make you feel inferior without your consent." —*Eleanor Roosevelt*

Vows

Love, Honor and Obey … That is what we‘re told
And, in the heat of passion we are truly sold!
We wear our stripes with honor and raise our families proud
We hide our life's ambitions behind a tearful shroud

Then we start to wonder? What will become of ME?
We lose our sense of *thunder* and no more can we see
Our face begins to wrinkle our hair will start to gray
Our butts and breasts they falter as gravity makes way

But, then the youth inside us begins to *Re-emerge*
As we leave our insecurity with confidence we splurge
The sheath of doubt now leaves us the butterfly is *Free*
For our wisdom it has aged it allows us too just *Be!*

Our spouse's will soon see us for *who* we have become
Our lives will grow together like thimbles on a thumb!
For as we're reunited the pretense is all gone!
We will love for who we are and not what we've put on!

Power Woman

We see the *Wives* that come and go
Deceived by … awesome splendors
As seasons pass and children grow
Their souls begin to plunder
But as they find themselves again …

They flow with silent wonder
Who is this Queen who slept so long?
Emerging life triumphant … From strength she rose
To conquer her woes … her fears and all her blunders
And, now she stands with shoulders high …

The *Mistress* of her pleasures …
As she grasped she found her equal ground
Then, with both her arms extended …
She received her mate with *truth* not fate
And welcomed their *mutual* treasures!

As children we were taught to accept the adults in our lives as the beings who could do no wrong, or at least they never had to explain when they were wrong. After all, they were the authorities who had the answers, and even if they didn't children were led to believe that they did. This paved the way to a false and protective world where we inherited their fears of failure and their insecurities of being found out. We adopted strong beliefs regarding our ability to accomplish goals and achieve aspirations. It also provided a multitude of excuses when we failed, and even exempted us from trying for fear of failing.

Children should recognize that we are all ordinary people who make mistakes, and that these mistakes don't necessarily need to be viewed as bad, but rather as stepping stones. Then they might not be as disappointed when they fall short of their goals. To paraphrase Thomas Edison, who stated to a reporter when asked how it felt about his 20,000 failed attempts to make the light bulb: "I didn't fail 20,000 times in making a light bulb. I now know 20,000 ways not to make one." By changing his paradigm, he not only took ownership of his unsuccessful attempts, but gracefully took credit for his success. By admitting to our mistakes, we teach our children not only humility, but accountability as well. What are we afraid of? The truth is supposed to set us free. Yet if it does not fit exactly into the mold that society has set, we feel obligated to re-pour the mold.

Adults are people, too. Perhaps it's time to drop the belief that once we reach a certain age we have all the answers. Respect is required and must be earned, not taken for granted, which is often the case.

Jerald's parents were separated when he was a young boy. He lived with his mother in his grandparent's house, where he was reminded on a daily basis that he had to respect his grandfather. Unfortunately, his grandfather was an alcoholic who belittled and demeaned Jerald. His self esteem was so shattered that when he dealt with his peers he presented himself as a tough guy, always getting into fights. As he got older, he fell into his grandfather's self-destructive pattern of alcohol and verbal abuse, entering into one failed relationship after another.

"Everything that irritates us about others can lead us to a better understanding of ourselves." – Carl Jung

Delusion or Confusion

My mind it does deceive me in a whirlpool of Confusion?
I follow what I am told to do … in a childish Delusion!
I think I'm like a Monkey, or a Squirrel might be like me
Always looking for new answers jumping from tree to tree
I won't recognize my weakness as yours come into view
For they're the ones I'll deal with because they belong to you
Perhaps when I take possession of what belongs to me
My mind will leave this maze I've built and see some Harmony
A change, a new perception, that's what I need for me
I'm fashioned like a bulldozer or an earthworm moving free
I'll travel through this world of mine …
Pushing boulders to the side …
And handle my addictions with *Dignity and Pride!*
I chose them as a lesson although not clear to me?
Once I take possession there is a cure in store for me
I see this as my weakness from which I'll surly grow
I'll stop blaming all the others for things that I should know
Now when I go shopping this isle I'll ignore …
For it puts me in a place … I do not need anymore
So often I would feel good …
But for a short time that would be …
And when the feeling wore off … I was slapped with *Reality!*
I used this as a crutch I allowed it to serve me
I fed it for my purpose enjoyed it temporarily…
And as I said before, when this feeling did wear off
My body gave me signals … For I'd throw up or just cough
I have all of my answers but refused sometimes to see
If I wallowed in this cesspool shame would be one with me!
There is a comfort deep inside me wanting to be free
But will not release the shackles until I respond with ability
I have no one to look to … It's my fault… this is clear
If I am to love again I must *release* myself from fear!

Viking

I am the manly Viking the *All* the power that is!
I watch my family cower as I holler at my kids …
My chest the case that holds emotions is caged inside its bars
And Oh! It is my Heart that dwells not in Venus but in Mars!
Anger roars like *thunder*! It strikes with lightening bolts!

But then I see your eyes, the portals to your Soul
And as I look inside them … My tears I can't control
For it's there I put the fear and pain I won't console
The truth of my affliction, awakes from quiet slumber
I can't reveal my love for it might expose my blunders

I used controlling thoughts to create a feeble brain
Now, I must release them along with all my pain
It's clear and quite apparent if I'm to be set free
I must admit to my mistakes and take responsibility!
Well, this is a new concept. At least it is for me

To be quiet and still communicate will be quite a feat you see
For I've always been so boisterous …
In fact quite forceful I could be… Yes, its time for changes …
With guidance from above I'll drop this false demeanor
And , *Alas* I'll find true love …

For years Vicky feared her father's wraith, yet when he was dying of cancer she chose to be with him for the last six weeks of his life. She came to know the vulnerable human being and fearful inner child he had been hiding for so many years. When she mentioned to others that her father was an alcoholic, she often got a reaction of "Oh, you poor thing! It must have been rough." She said on one level it was, but that her father's addiction taught her the path that she didn't want for herself. As a teenager and young adult, she tried using alcohol to solve her problems, medicating herself. She thought it would make her insecurities go away, but to her dismay it only made things worse. She would wake up with a splitting headache, not remembering the night before and not knowing if she really wanted to face her friends. She decided that not being in control of her facilities was a lot worse than just facing the problem at hand.

Her mother dealt with her insecurities by using the guilt train, and she sold tickets on every corner. While fancying herself as being orthodox and polite, she hid behind a shroud of insecurities, blanketed by her own fear of rejection. She managed to keep a safe emotional distance from her family and friends. Apparently, both of Vicky's parents had addictions to contend with. Fortunately, Vicky was able to recognize that if they had been able to get the guidance they needed, they might have come to terms with their use of emotional crutches. During her childhood, mental and emotional health care was a luxury that could only be afforded by the wealthy. Luckily, with all of the self help books, seminars, workshops, and programs out today, that is no longer the case.

Although the process is slow, people like Vicky are beginning to seek out the appropriate guidance that not only conforms to their personal comfort zone, but crosses the boundaries of social and religious taboos. Hopefully, we will all begin to respect each other's individuality. Rather than blame others for our poor choices, or blame the devil, we need to recognize that we are ultimately responsible. We must exercise our free will to make our own choices. Punishment is not God's will, but consequences are, and only when we take ownership of our deeds will we be free of shame.

"Hate the sin not the sinner." —Mahatma Gandhi

Know "Me" for who I am!

If you really knew me
You would listen, look and hear!
You would see my loud aggression
Is really only *Fear*
If you really knew me
You would look into my eyes
They are the clouded mirrors
Concealing all the lies
A clown that always smiles
For someone else to see
Will hide its true emotions
And throw away the key

It is time to share my essence
The fibers of my Soul
A Soul that longs to love you
When Ego's lost control
The issue is not bondage
It is sharing the all that is
The *Joy, the Pain the Patience*
The loving that one gives
This love it has no pretense
It is always here
If you look into my eyes
You will see how much *I Care!*

RIGIDITY
ANGER
IGNORANCE
FEAR
GREED
HYPOCRISY
ADDICTION

Sins of the Father

I have never met your Father but still I knew him well
As he indulged in his addictions our lives became a *Hell*
Like devils through the ages we'll share their destiny
Unless we choose to blow apart the mask of *Blasphemy!*

Our, Mothers, like theirs before them …
All hid in quiet shame the fear that brewed inside them
Would shoulder all the blame …
Ignorance ... it drove them to follow as before

Now that we're enlightened it has opened up the door
The voice of *Spirit* guides us the fear has gone away
Responsibility, it is my name I wear it everyday!
It has taught me strength and freedom all new rules to the game

The dogma that I followed set many limits to claim
My middle name is *Choice* now, of that I am real clear!
My path is not, prediction, addiction … Nor is it fear
Integrity... will drive me it is the name I'll hold so Dear!

Family morals and values have been so severally shattered by today's fast pace, that we're becoming a "Do as I say, *not* as I do society." Are we accountable for our actions or are we just going through the motions? Have our social myths, cultures, inherited belief systems, religions, gangs, clubs, charity organizations, and other group associations led us into the preverbal box? When traveling through history, we find that these unfortunate happenings are not new to man's behavior or cultures. It began with two brothers whose rivalry was so competitive that it ended in murder, and continued with pharos and kings, dictators and czars. Today it is still perpetuated by neighborhood gangs, whose families chose the path of jealousy and hatred to create their perceptions of the perfect world. We might discover that the root to all evil is not necessarily money or lust, but perhaps it's **E**dging **G**od **O**ut; the need to be in complete control of not only our lives, but of all those around us. If we were to take control of what is only ours to master, we might find that there is no time to swim in another's pool.

Instead, we have allowed our fears and feelings of guilt to guide us into chaos. I do not subscribe to the thought that any one specific culture or philosophy is the answer to solving the ills of the world. I know that there is only one race, the human race, and if we don't begin to respect each other we will certainly destroy ourselves. If we are ever to experience real peace on earth, we must first have the insight to accept reality as what is real. By this I mean not pointing fingers at others for our problems and then forcing our solutions on them. We must be willing to take ownership, thus creating a new reality.

We are becoming a culture full of excuses and quick fixes. If our children are misbehaving, we immediately assume they are suffering from some form of chemical imbalance. Almost invariably they are diagnosed with ADHD, ADD, Bi-polar or XYZ, and in some cases the prescribed drugs can help a child focus. However, I am sad to say that in all too many cases the disorders could have been remedied by carefully monitoring the diet and giving the child plain old attention. Children need attention, and they will find it any way they can. Because of this super charged pace we live in, more and more parents are finding it extremely difficult to supply the quality time and attention that their children need. As a result, they are either medicated by some mood altering drug that turns a normally inquisitive and active child into a zombie, or they are mesmerized by the television or another video game. Very few children even go outdoors unless they are forced.

Another unfortunate truth is that with so many single parents these days, the children are being put on hold so the parents can join the dating game. If another partner becomes part of the family, the children are not always accepted or vice versa. This situation makes for a very difficult way of life and sends some damaging messages to our children about two parent households.

Andrea's mother, Beverly, would spike Andrea's formula with Nyquil in order to put her to sleep quickly. As Andrea got older, Beverly consulted several pediatricians until she finally found one who gave her a prescription for Ritalin to control her daughter's constant chatter.

Now in her early 20s, Andrea is taking several mood altering medications. She feels they are necessary because she simply cannot focus for longer than 30 minutes at a time.

While attending an anger management class, she revealed that she was out of pills and had not taken one for nearly a week. Once she started to practice meditation, she was able to focus quite comfortably, and she started a new job that really interested her. She also started to date a young man who was genuinely interested in spending time with her.

I would never suggest to a client that they just stop their medications cold turkey, but one should consider seeking a physician who does not routinely prescribe medication as the cure-all solution. Good advice might be to find one who would suggest other alternative means of satisfying ones nervousness or anxieties by the use of exercise, meditation, herbal supplements, yoga and the like. As a society, we have become way too dependent on quick fixes, rather than working out a problem or situation through thought and concentration.

"We don't receive wisdom, we must discover it for ourselves after a journey that no one can take for us or spare us."– Marcel Proust

ADHD

Today you sit in judgment and most of it for me!
You treat me like a burden, a parasite, a flea
I fell into your caldron a witch's brew at best
You were the black widow, I fell victim to your nest
How dare you be so righteous to put the blame on me!
I was your babe your infant …
You were supposed to take care of me!
You fed me all the medicine so quiet I would be
And blamed all my activity on … ADHD!
The fact is I was normal a child like all others …
It wasn't really my fault that I was not one of the brothers!
If I were born a boy how different would life be?
Perhaps! Dad would have stayed and a Mother you would be
To bad you are my parent … That was a big mistake
For now it's real apparent … This roll you did not take
At first the only feeling that I could touch was hate
You left me all alone so you could have a date!
But, now I see your weakness was an inherent part of you
You acted like your Mother and then your Grand Ma too
If all that we were taught is that there is no real Value!
Then how are we to break that awful chain in two?
You hid me for a while till I got wise to you!
Then you let me do. Whatever I wanted to
Now that I'm in trouble and, out here in clear view
The responsibility is *ours* to seek good counsel too
Of course it won't be easy to *share* this blame with you
But, if we don't do this together we'll shrink right out of view!
Much like an old rock star lost in their past fame
Our lessons must be learned or *disgrace* will be our Name!

Trust

Trust it is a judgment … a call not all can make
For some they may just borrow … and others will just take
We seek all the attention and notoriety …
But, fail to see the consequence for our lack of … Integrity!
Our word should be a *bond* not, one of paper made
It comes straight from the Soul with support and *Spirits* aid
To others we may lie … we may steal or we may cheat!
But look into our eyes you will see there is defeat
I thought you could be trusted a mistake on my behalf
One you took advantage of as you walked away and laughed
For now you are the winner the holder of the prize
Look into the mirror and you'll see who you despise?
Your lies they may have hurt me of this I will admit
But it's *You* who dug the hole and fell into the pit …
You saw these desperate measures as a road you had to take
Too bad you did not realize … *I love you for God sake!*
I will always try to help you no matter what you do
When I look into your eyes … I see an Angel crying too
I know that you've been hurt but it's not beyond repair
So go directly to your heart there is *Forgiveness* there
I know that you're afraid … of rejection and some scorn
Please know that God is with you …
He is here from … Dusk to Dawn!

There is hardly a day that you can pick up a newspaper or turn on the radio or television without hearing something about Paris Hilton, Brittany Spears or some other wealthy debutant or pop star making a complete ass of themselves because of their out of control addictions. I'm not talking about addictions to alcohol or drugs or even sex. I'm talking about the addiction to attention and unhappiness. If these celebrities did not want to be in the lime light they could change the circumstances. The truth is they are addicted to the attention drawn to them by the slightest indiscretion.

As a result, we are teaching our young adults and even their parents that it is fine to disrespect authority. If you are a young adult, you can blame your troubles on the lack of parental discipline. If you are an adult authority figure, you can blame it on the government, the church, the problems you are having with your children, your spouse, your boss, the stock market, interest rates, and on and on. Telling the truth is an option only used if you see yourself coming out on the upside of a situation. If not, then it is socially acceptable to tell "a little white lie." After all, you are only doing it to save someone else from embarrassment or getting their feelings hurt.

This adopted philosophy only perpetuates the downward spiral of deception and dishonesty. The sad thing is that it has become a widely accepted behavior which is often not recognized until someone is hurt or the people closest to us have been run off. We lie to ourselves while carefully weaving a web of denial around our sensitive egos. We use excuses like rationalization, stating that if someone else had taken care of a particular chore or duty, we would not have gotten upset or angry. Rather than being responsible for what is ours, we find it so much easier to pass it forward. After all, if you look bad, I will look so much better.

Have you ever misplaced your wallet and looked all over the house for it? And then once you feel you have exhausted all your energy, you accuse one of the children or your spouse of misplacing the wallet. You make a complete ass of yourself by ranting and raving because someone else in the house had to have been responsible for moving it. Then you find it in the pocket of your pants, but rather than acknowledging your mistake, you sheepishly go on with your business, leaving a trail of frustration behind you and very possibly creating chaos for the entire day. And we wonder why our family won't confide in us? Could it be for fear of our reaction?

The solution is to acknowledge and then take responsibility for every one of our irresponsible actions so we can move forward with change. For years my husband and I ran a construction business. We would hire and fire young people on a weekly basis, either because they lied about their experience or they just didn't want to work. As much as we hated this constant turn over, the truth was that most people today don't feel any obligation to work. Unless they start at the top of the ladder, making huge money and driving a company vehicle, they would rather live off the system. Life has become one big party and the price is becoming more and more apparent every day.

"We cannot always build the future for our youth but we can build our youth for our future." – *Franklin D Roosevelt*

Friday Night

Friday night, could be considered by some a special night
It is the ending of a work week with a party in clear sight
Now some may wash their hair or reflect upon the week
Not me I want to party. I'm eighteen and at my peek!
I choose my girlfriends carefully we are Divas all the same
We trade our bras and panty hose and our make-up is a game
Then once we are all ready we go out on the town
We dance in our stilettos bringing *Mr. Six Pack* to the ground!

Now we'll have our boundaries but rules! Well there are none!
Once we're on the loose, we're like, Annie with her gun!
Perhaps, I may seem shallow but, No, this isn't true
I'll share my *Mr. Six Pack* with you and you and you!
Some Friday nights might differ there's some we might reflect!
We wash our hair and paint our toes …
And trash the cloths that we reject …
This time it may seem wasted but, Oh no, that isn't true…

You see the next day is Saturday and that is a great night to!

Teens

When I was a teen my *Dad* was so mean I had to run away!
I thought that life was just a game and I just had to play
What I could see was *only* me and the things I did all day
You closed my doors and gave me chores
"Be Responsible" you'd say!
I didn't see you wanted me to be mature, then go on my way
My eyes were *Blind* ... but I did not mind …
I fought you in every way I knew it all and I had a ball
The crazy things I'd say I broke your heart as we grew apart
But now I'm here to stay you were not wrong I do belong
My friends I thought they cared for me …
How could I've been so wrong?
They fed me drugs and alcohol then sold me for a song!
The times were fun or so I thought for I always went along
When told to sell I went to hell for now I can't get off
It hooked me bad I was always sad until I got a fix
Oh my GOD please … *look...* at me! I feel one hundred six
I sniffed it here and shot it there it made me feel so good
And when I woke the whole town spoke …
I was the thief of the neighborhood …
I won't accept this awful fate it's a new choice I must make
So with boundaries set and a *Safety Net!*
I will choose a different fate I reach to you who made me view
That a change is not too late …
I see it now and draw on it I welcome your support
And with your help I can be free to repossess my integrity
I must no longer be the jerk who was lost so long ago
As my wounds do heal my scars reveal …
The things I thought *weren't* wrong
For now I know if I'm to grow …
I must *release* all blame to be strong!

I've got a thought. How about looking at the plight of our families without pointing fingers at the system and its social ills? For decades we have not only raped our land but our family values as well. How did this happen? Why do so many women feel that in order to live they must have a man to support them? Not just financially, but emotionally, too. And why do so many men feel that the only way they can keep their manhood is by brow beating their women and robbing them of their self esteem? Perhaps if these questions were addressed honestly, the divorce rate would not be as high and families would not be on the endangered species list.

It's no wonder that so many couples are living together without a real commitment. An all too common practice is to get a partner, try him or her out, and if they don't suit your fancy, get rid of them. How can we be so dependent and yet so cocky? It seems as though both sides want to have their cake and eat it too. What happened to getting to know a person before making a life time commitment? We yield to the passion of the moment and allow our common sense to fall into a coma, only to wake up one day, wondering how we arrived at this uncomfortable state of mind. We should acknowledge the fact that our insecurities and fears are the culprits, and our unwillingness to relinquish our control could lead to our demise.

As a result, we repeat patterns and allow our fears to block any thoughts of making a change. We stay in the proverbial box, stuck and confused, while watching our children and families end in disaster, using the excuse that it just didn't work out. Is this true, or is it that we were too stubborn to reach a compromise?

The good news is that once we open our minds, the choice is made to create a change. Our lives begin to fill with new possibilities. The even better news is that when we start living the new possibilities, our friends and loved ones can't help but wonder how this change came about, and they begin to open up to change as well. It's a win-win situation. The ultimate question is: Are we willing to work for a positive change, or have we become so self-absorbed that our worlds are only being observed from one side?

"We could never learn to be brave and patient, if there were only joy in the world. I do not want the peace which passeth understandings, I want the understanding which bringeth peace." —Helen Keller

A New Chapter

You came into our lives so many years ago
Enriched our hearts and spirits despite all of your woe
You've grown into a *woman* from a cuddly little girl
And now you're getting ready … To go out into the world!
I know this time is frightening and exciting too!
Remember that we're here for you
Too help and guide you through
Always look for goodness in everything you do
And God will be beside you if you deal with what is true

While this is a new chapter one you're yet to write
If you keep your, *wit and wisdom…*
Your soul will take great flight …
No matter what has happened be it good or bad …
Leave the past behind you the future is your *New Path!*
OH! So many lessons you have yet to learn …
Like chapters in a book these stories your will Earn
And as you read your stories keep in mind each day
That life is one big theater and we are just *actors* in this play

As problems are presented
You will have the *choice!*
To keep them all inside you …
Or express them with your voice …
Once you've shared your challenge it will become real clear!
Your answers are inside you so let go of your Fear!
Trust that God is with you … Although, you might not see
He will lift up all your spirits
To bring you Peace, Happiness and Glee!

Value

Like coal is to a diamond I have watched you Grow
A woman you're becoming from your head right to your toe
We all know that you're cunning a budding star it's true
The Jewel you are will shine by far as it glistens in ones view

Your life is just a proving ground with judgments from the past
While immature you'll grow for sure …
These foolish games won't last
Soon you'll see the levity that forgiveness will always cast!

Forgive you this… *Forgive* you that but hold on to no wrong
As you let go you'll free your *SOUL*
And with love you will have grown
Your goodness shines like starry eyes on velvet blue black skies

Of this I am sure! Your heart is pure and that no one denies
With love you'll see the pleasantry a warm heart can supply
For as you grow you'll surely know …
That… true love will not lie!

For years Jenna's family argued with her, trying to persuade her to move from the West coast to the East coast, where most of her family lived. The general feeling was that in her declining years she needed to be closer to the family to provide the care she would eventually need. However, Jenna did not see it that way. After all, she had established a life with many friends and hobbies and enjoyed her life right where she was. At first her family could not understand, and thought she was just being stubborn. However, they finally conceded to her wishes and discontinued their insistence. They realized that while the move would be easier on them, it would not necessarily be in the best interest of Jenna. So it was her choice to live where she wanted. Everyone eventually agreed that until it was impossible for Jenna to care for herself, she would stay right where she was. And when the time came, she would have to be moved. Well, they would cross that bridge when they came to it.

Families often think they're doing what's best for their elderly parents by taking control, yet those elderly parents are perfectly capable of handling their own affairs. This is similar to well meaning parents who attempt to take charge of their adult children and siblings, wishing they would conform to what they feel is a right choice for their lives. Why do we think we have the right to sail someone else's ship? Is it possibly because we're not sure of our own direction? Or if we allow someone to follow their dreams and they succeed, we fear that we might be viewed as a failure for not pursuing our own dreams? This is one of the mysteries of life. If we were to find the answer, we would most likely have to face our ego and let go.

"The shoe that fits one person pinches another; there is no recipe for living that suits all cases." —Carl Jung

Distant Mother

You stayed away so long … A mother you could not be
I don't know what the reason it made no sense to me
You said it was your health. But its fear I thinking of
For years you hid inside yourself afraid to show your love

It was a shame because we missed you. So many miles away
You couldn't know your family your pride kept you at bay
So now you are old and weary I fear it is too late
Because you can not travel and our commitments are to great

So many years were wasted to serve a foolish pride
Perhaps, we'll see you again one day?
When we cross to the other side I hope that then you'll tell us
Why it was so hard to be a part of us and our families too

Please don't think we're complaining for this we can not do
We realize you were doing what you thought was best for you
Despite our disappointment we want to share with you
We love you you're our *Mother* no matter what you do

Just know that we do miss you and think of you most ways
We hope that you are happy right to your final days
Although, we're not together and our bodies may not touch
Our Souls will bond forever …

You're our Mother to us that means so much!

Andrew was strong, hardworking, and dedicated to his family. As a child he grew up during the Depression, so having a job was of the utmost importance. Education was only for the rich. He had four sons, who he pushed into the work force as soon as they were able bodied. He never considered the importance of an education; he felt that as long as you got a paycheck at the end of every week, life was good. His son Jonathan was smart, witty, and eager to learn. However, the family was so poor that Jonathon barely made it to school, as his father was constantly taking him along to his job. While he was always clean, Jonathan was often ridiculed and embarrassed by his ratty looking clothes and long hair. When he approached his parents about taking up a school sport, they would look at him as though he had ten heads, saying that they had no money for rich kid games.

Jonathon and his Dad would frequently banter back and forth, using sarcastic humor to communicate their views and opinions. Outsiders would often look at them in confusion, not knowing if they were kidding. All too often, we pass judgment without even the slightest understanding of the particular circumstances. I think it's important to view people as though you were watching a movie, by separating each character and each role. And then place yourself in the individual roles, so you can see the true picture. It might be a surprise just how quickly you release your judgment.

The time Jonathan spent with his father was often frustrating, but always peppered with mild antidotes that were laced with humor. For years Jonathan held a quiet resentment toward his father for not allowing him to pursue an education. He left home as a teenager and swore he would never return. As fate would have it, when Andrew was no longer capable of caring for himself, Jonathan became his full time caretaker. He was faced with a soul searching dilemma. His internal battle was a daily trial, as he was caught between harboring his resentment and coming to grips with it, possibly even releasing it.

To his amazement, Jonathan came to understand his father's reasoning for what he had perceived as a lack of ambition. He discovered that this attitude stemmed from Andrew's own feelings of inadequacy. He was not only a product of the depression, but he had little education of his own, for he had been thrown into the work force at age 11. He feared that if his boys were to get an education, they would no longer look up to him; their success might lead them away from him. Both men failed to see that this fear of inadequacy and abandonment was the force that created the gap in their relationship.

Jonathan became a successful businessman with a family of his own. One day, Jonathan took Andrew to a job with him. He had stacked some debris and pieces of scrap wood at the exit door to be taken to the trash. Andrew picked it up to take outside when Jonathan, in a loud voice, told Andrew to put it down before he hurt himself. Andrew felt helpless and became upset.

But as soon as Jonathan was distracted, Andrew proceeded to remove the stack from the house. By the time Jonathan realized what had happened, the wood was gone.

When he asked Andrew where the wood went, Andrew asked, "What wood?"

Jonathan said "The wood, Dad. Where did you put the wood that I had stacked in the corner?"

With a slight twinkle in his eye, Andrew said, "If you're so smart, you find it!" At that point Jonathan wanted to strangle his Dad, but he realized it would do no good to be angry. So he rummaged around and noticed that on the side of the house there were pieces of white wood sticking out of the shrubbery. Andrew had carefully placed them in the palmetto trees on the vacant lot next door. For those who don't know what a palmetto tree is, it's a small palm tree with nasty barbs that grows wild in Florida. Needless to say, Jonathan was less than happy while retrieving the wood. Andrew, on the other hand, sat quietly in the work van, drinking a soda.

When Jonathan returned to the van after picking up the trash, Andrew gave him a blank stare and said, "Where have you been, Son?"

Biting his lip, Jonathan replied, "Nowhere, Dad. I've been nowhere."

As he drove back to the shop, Jonathan started to chuckle, thinking about the incident. Then he broke into an uncontrollable belly laugh. Andrew joined in the laughter, and soon both men were in tears as they made their way back to the shop. Jonathan knew that if he lost his sense of humor, he would probably not be able to continue caring for his dad. It was difficult for him to watch this once powerful man slowly deteriorate to a childlike state.

We can often become insensitive to the feelings of the elderly by failing to appreciate how difficult it must be for them to change roles, especially when they're suffering from Dementia or Alzheimer's disease. We must keep in mind that our lessons are always on-going. There will be a day when our own role will change. If we don't teach our future caregivers compassion and tolerance, we will definitely suffer the consequences.

"An understanding heart is everything in a teacher, and cannot be esteemed highly enough. One looks back with appreciation to the brilliant teachers, but with gratitude to those who touched our human feeling. The curriculum is so much necessary raw material, but warmth is the vital element for the growing plant and for the soul of the child." —*Carl Jung*

Old Timers

I'm old and can't remember
The things that I once could

But it doesn't really matter
Because, it never did much good

I nagged and then complained
But no one would hear or listen

Now when I don't remember
I won't mention it … You see

For I know it will drive you crazy
Just like you did to me!

Aging Together

The things that I've forgotten may all be new to you?
You think you are so clever as you are growing too
You should listen to your elders but that's not what you'll do
The lessons you are learning are so hard to pursue

Perhaps instead of argue we should *"Communicate"*
Before we form a blockade through which we can't relate
Our age it is a factor and temperaments are too
They may not be so welcome. Oh, what are we to do?

The facts of life might change us we know that this is true
Depression could destroy us if we don't get a Clue?
Our parts they are not working as well as they used too
Our brains are getting slower our eyes are losing view

When I look into the mirror, I see not only you
I see a part of me that is also shining through
We hide within our fears a complicated shrew
This Confusion will destroy us if we don't clear the view

I will admit in my confessions to all the wrongs I've done
But, responsibility for yours, well of that I will take none!
As we look for our great demons *Fear* is number one!
It limits our evolvement and reduces it to a crumb

If we're to rise above the chaos then this we'd better do
You tell the truth to me and I'll tell the truth to you!
Talking face to face that's what we must do
And stay away from Gossip that is often so Un-true!

Crazy Family

I chose this *crazy* family I was placed here as a guide
I will expose the inhibitions that come from deep inside
They grew from faulty systems beliefs sold all as truths
And soon became defenses as good as *chicken hoofs*

We dress them in their costumes and put them on display
And hope they'll be accepted as pleasures for the day
But soon to our chagrin reality comes to stay
We must face these *foolish* games and send them on their way

If we're to learn our lessons we must begin to tell the truth
We must value our integrity as more the just a spoof
For if we thrive on our excuses our lives will have become
As *lame* as our defenses so as not to face them we will run

If we would view the mirrors that reveal our blatant lies
We might recognize these demons that give no *compromise*
We might salvage our good families before it is too late
With a whole new way of thinking we will *communicate!*

Some people believe in Karma and reincarnation. They have an understanding that souls enter this incarnation seeking to learn from the challenges of past lives. Whether this is your belief or not is irrelevant. The point is that we are here now, and we do have lessons to be learned, as well as teach, either for a past life, or from our past in this life. These lessons are being presented everyday.

We often find ourselves getting angry over the slightest things and wonder why. We do not realize that our subconscious minds are storage cabinets. We react to a facial expression, tone of voice, certain body language, and we display a reaction of anger. We do not often understand the trigger that stemmed from someone leaving a negative mark on our psyche. We tend to suppress these negative events in our subconscious minds. Then one day, when someone says something or does something, it's *Ka-boom!* We explode in anger and confusion, while embedding our hurts and fears even deeper into the caverns of our subconscious minds.

Rather than reacting with fits of anger or repression, we might consider changing our thoughts, as well as our paradigms. In order to do this, we will need some guidance, education, or training.

In his book "Living the Seven Habits," Stephen Covey offers his description of two roles: one as a guide and the other as a teacher. The guide is the one who takes you to unfamiliar places, making it possible for you to see other choices and new experiences. The teacher will point out different angles or entirely new ways of looking at the choices, thus enhancing your understanding and perceptions. The following story poems will provide a few simple tips to assist you in remembering quick solutions to handling your anger, before irreparable damage is done. Use them as guides.

As Socrates pointed out to his friend, who was so eager to share local gossip, "Before you repeat something make sure you can pass the triple filter test. First, is it true? Second, is it something good? And third, is it of any use?"

I'm sure we have all experienced tidbits of local gossip, which later blew up and caused all manner of chaos. Or we've been approached by someone wanting advice, and rather than allowing the person to solve their own problem, we offer *our* answers or worse yet, we contribute by agreeing or taking sides, making the situation even worse than it was in the beginning.

In my anger management workbook "Shut the Duck Up," I describe this as a duck farm. That's when we are supposed to be listening, but we are often busy formulating our own solutions. We don't allow the other party to work out their own problems. People sometimes just need to vent!

"Human beings, by changing the inner attitudes of their mind, can change the outer aspects of their lives." – William James

Shut the Duck Up!

When I first arrived here I purchased a small *Duck!*
I fed it my opinions and gradually it grew
It had all of the answers … for me and then for you
I listened quite intently as judgment it did pass!

It made me feel superior while you were just an … *Ass!*
I fed it while I listened as my answers were a clue
It soon became a flock projecting only my point of view
Then soon I was to learn a bitter lesson or two

For while I fed my Duck … I wasn't listening to you
So now I will go hunting I'll find myself a Gun!
Point it at the flock and the Duck will be on the Run
My lessons are so many they overflow my cup

But, the one of most importance is
to "SHUT THE DUCK UP!"

Breathe

When you start to breathe
The air goes in then out
The difference is the time you take
To release or maybe *Shout!*

For those intervening seconds
A short time to conclude
Could surely make the difference
In your Life… and… *Attitude!*

It is that space in time
That only you create
A buffer zone a cushioned place
Where anger can… *Sedate!*

Perhaps? You might slow down
And take a moment or two!
To look and then evaluate
Another… *Point of View!*

Opinions

My life is full of Pleasure and then there is the Pain!
An emotion I stay away from for it fills me full of Shame
My mind begins to wonder and soon my heart will follow
Gossip! It consumes me and makes me live in Squalor!
This idle little chit chat keeps… *Quacking like a Duck!*

It consumes my common sense I start acting like a cluck!
At times I will ignore it but that's often not the case
My logic will escape me *Gossip!* Sends it on a Chase
It's the times that I *don't* listen that my soul is truly Free!
To make my own decisions and not just cop a Plea

The Truth is that I'm hunting a proper place for me
For that's the place I'm setting so with comfort I can be
I've come to the conclusion although it's just a Clue
The things that I'm eluding are keeping me from you
The change I need to make now is one of *ATTITUDE!*

I've made all the excuses I'm often considered rude
It's time to take Possession it's me that does intrude
So, from now on as I listen to other points of view
I will recognize these *Belly Buttons* like me you have one too
OH! Yes, it's your opinion and it does belong to *YOU!*

Anger is a thinking game, not an emotion. We wake up in the morning, planning our day. When exposed to someone or something that just rubs us the wrong way, we tend to overreact. We have just entered the Duck Farm; our little voices are just a quackin'. Then we feed them even more by using our defense mechanisms and irrational feelings. We take many remarks directed at us as personal affronts, as we proceed to internalize them, filing them away, only to fortify and support our flock with excuses.

When I conduct an anger management workshop, I always encourage the students to create an emotional tool box. This consists of a list of people who will tell you what you *need* to hear, not what you want to hear. Then you're encouraged to review the incident by breaking it down step by step. This allows you to recognize your slice of the pie. At this time, it is important to be brutally honest with yourself. That's why it is so important to have another person assist you in identifying your anger, rather than rationalizing it.

I will further address that not all anger is harmful. If anger is channeled to promote positive change, it can make all the difference in the world. However, our first responsibility is to ourselves, being accountable for our own actions. It is the only way we will break our ancestral chains of fear, shame, blame, and guilt. These feelings were passed to us by well meaning parents, teachers, and preachers, and while they may have wanted the best for us, their best may not have been our best.

"Speak when you are angry and you will make the best speech you will ever regret."
– Dr. Peter J Laurence.

Disappointed

I feel so *disappointed* for what's been done to me
My *hurt* and my *confusion* have driven me to be
An angry, cranky person who simple will not see
That all of this *frustration* is what I brought on ME!
I perceived it as *harassmen*t and took it personally!
Then with great *annoyance* you wouldn't hear my plea
I asked you for *forgiveness* as I filed internally …
All the pain that you dished out I made it part of me
I held on to *repression* and joked along the way
Hiding my *true feelings* with silence everyday
Projecting my *rejection* and giving it to you!
I clearly saw your faults while mine were all too *few!*
Perhaps I need to focus on what I have become
A whining little child who needs to suck my thumb!
For when you took me shopping I missed an isle of two
I noticed that your happiness was coming into view
Then when you took *possession* of what belonged to you
Your *freedom* from repression came with honesty its true
I envied this new freedom for I hoped that I would too
Find the Guts the Chutzpah to take the same avenue
For then I'm sure to *recognize* my life is up to me
To see my faults for what they are and accept what I can be
The blame it is so easy to shift to other shoulders
Like standing top a cliff and throwing off the boulders
There were times I did not see that selfish part of me
I preyed on that enabling part of your personality
It made *you* feel so guilty and I would get my way
But, what I was not seeing is that I pushed you far away!
For this I am real sorry and I do *apologize!*
I put myself before all others without any *compromise*
Perhaps, I didn't realize or just didn't want to see
That your feelings were as important as the ones I had for *ME!*

Spinning Wheel

Life, is like a spinning wheel
Turning round and round
When it's out of c*ontrol!*
It will throw you to the ground!

I know I need to follow
Its spokes right to the center
For there I'll find my balance
A *peace* that's free to enter!

I'll focus on important things
The small things they won't matter
I will choose the ones with meaning
Not those with idle chatter!

Gossip! Is a foe to me
It hurts all those concerned
It kills off the integrity
That I have so hard earned

When I look inside myself
I can plainly see
The *Angels* looking through my eyes
Are looking back at *ME!*

When people hold positions of authority, whether it is in the workplace or in the home, they tend to feel that it gives them license to force their will on another, who may not be as financially or emotionally secure and to stand up for themselves. When this happens, the dominant personality frequently overlooks the fact that if a relationship is going to work, there must be respect.

Statistics show that business productivity increases when there is a sense of loyalty toward employers. It has also been proven that when an employee is treated with dignity, no matter what the position they hold, there is less office gossip and back stabbing. Unfortunately, the practice of respect is not often displayed in the home. This leaves our work force no alternative but to bring their patterned behaviors into their occupations.

This destructive pattern can only be addressed by example and education, which might explain the increasing percentage of people who jump from one job to another with attitude chips on their shoulders. The myth that women must stay home and bake bread has obviously been all but obliterated in today's cultures because of our basic need to survive. Yet, the willingness of people to take a shared responsibility in both domestic and career obligations is sorely lacking. Our population is suffering from a severe case of arrogance through control, and submissiveness due to fear.

Successful partnerships must share responsibilities with a one hundred per cent commitment, meaning that while one partner might be contributing forty percent, the other is giving sixty, and as the wheel turns so do the percentages.

When Karen was in her early 20s, her husband Ken was attending college in the evenings. She stayed home during the week, but on the weekends she worked as a cocktail waitress until the early hours of the morning. Before she left for work she would make sure dinner was prepared and waiting in oven so Ken could eat with the children.

One night she came home from work feeling exhausted because there had been a convention in town, and her lounge was especially busy. When she walked into her kitchen she was faced with a sink full of dishes, and leftovers on the counters. Needless to say, she saw red. She was not only angry because of the mess, but also because of the apparent lack of respect, which left her feeling hurt and devalued. In the morning, she yelled at Ken for not cleaning up.

He responded, "It's not my job to clean up. I'm the man." This retort would ring in Karen's ears for years to come.

Ken had no idea of the depth of his insult. His lack of consideration was not only insulting, but demeaning. Ken could have avoided what eventually turned into deep resentment for him if he had only thought before he spoke. Instead, as the years passed, he continued to show his obvious lack of respect with indifference. Eventually, Karen had taken all that she could. Ken's disrespect eroded their relationship until it was almost too late.

As a last ditch attempt to save their relationship, Karen decided to seek counseling. She was advised to practice talking *to* Ken rather than at him. At first she felt awkward, but with practice she was able to open a line of communication.

If you find it hard to communicate with a partner, you may find that a good practice is to remove yourself from the scene until you can clear your mind. And then ask yourself if what you are feeling is a fair perception of the truth, or are you simply feeding your selfishness? Ask yourself how you would feel if the conflict didn't happen. You must be honest with your answers, or you will be wasting your time. Once you have established your true feelings, determine how to go about creating a change. This exercise will work only if you are completely honest and you are willing to put yourself in the hot seat with total truth. You may be capable of deceiving yourself, but if you are totally honest you will eventually discover your own lies.

"That you may retain your self-respect, it is better to displease the people by doing what you know is right, than to temporarily please them by doing what you know to be wrong." —William J.H. Boetcker

Cave Man

You say I want to argue that's all we ever do
And if I don't agree you see no other point of view
You say I took your manhood your valor and your pride
It was you that walked away and tossed our life aside
You say that I don't need you. Perhaps this might be true
I *want* the love and support we had …
The mature man I once knew…

I raised all of our children they filed out the door
Now please let me assure you I don't need any more
Hobbies are important this I understand
They serve the boy inside …
But let's not forget the man, put them in prospective
Or they will damage you, first we pay the bills
Then take time for you …

What is your direction, do you have a clue?
If we're to be together then we must start a new
What are your priorities? Am I included too?
Please rethink your promise …
Are our commitments both the same?
Or this relationship won't work, if we navigate with blame
These decisions must be made before I change my Name!

Letting Go

Who are these Mighty Humans?
GOD watches as they grow
Deceived by shallow motives
That corrode the sacred soul

Seasons, pass as children sow
Their souls begin to wonder
Ego rears its ugly head
And forages through like *Thunder!*

Souls will hide from what is dear
Alluding happiness because of fear
Due to guilt and then some blame
Pathways clearly paved with shame

We ask that SPIRIT guide us
To recognize our … truth
And now that we've *re-membered*
A changing world will be the proof

We rise with fearless pleasure
We made it to the stars
Now, one with heart and soul
We bring *Venus to bond with Mars…*

We are experiencing an epidemic of split families. It is quite a phenomenon to have a child in school with the same last name as both their parents. I was speaking to a young girl once who asked me if my children had the same father. I thought that it was a strange question; until she went on to explain that she had six siblings and three fathers. I never really gave it much thought, but upon investigation and observation, I can say that while the divorce rate may be declining, the number of single family households is not. Perhaps the divorce rate is declining because couples are simple not getting married.

It is all too common to have couples move in together to play house, yet when the going gets rough they split up. So where does this leave the children? Children from these relationships are frequently left confused, and are often used as pawns to gain emotional control or achieve financial gain. These all too common dysfunctional circumstances lead to future generations having distorted values and pessimistic beliefs about the inevitable failure of any family unit.

In the late 1980s, a friend of mine told about his son who had gotten his girlfriend pregnant. My friend, drawing on his fundamentalist background, advised his son to do the "right thing" by getting married and giving his girlfriend and their unborn child a legal name. Under a great deal of guilt and conviction, he did marry her. However, the relationship turned into a disaster. Both parities were too young; neither had a clue of how to handle the simplest of household responsibilities, and both were under the impression that if they could not meet their financial obligations, Mom and Dad would bail them out. Within two years, the marriage was further challenged by the appearance of another child. The one adult pleasure they did master soon turned into a total disaster. Consequently, the young man was satisfying his insatiable appetite all over town, while his young bride sat home with a great deal of resentment and hostility, not only toward her husband, but toward her two children. Their marriage ended in a bitter divorce, using the child visitation rights as a tool of manipulation for financial gain.

If a relationship doesn't work out between parents, they might be reminded that the children are not responsible for the choices made by their parents. Love should be their legacy, not revenge.

"There is no revenge so complete as forgiveness." —*Josh Billings*

Jilted Lover

I am the Jilted lover I've consumed myself with hate
I'll see you with no other I will curse you as you date
Although time has started passing. I will regurgitate
The true love we once had and breed it with more hate
Some say "I'm to forgive you". But that I will not do
You took my heart and destroyed it you've broken it in two
So now it's time to hurt you I think I'll take away
Our child that's my leverage I'll see you cry, you'll pay!
The Devil is my witness I'll wish all harm to you
Then Spirit came to save me I received his guiding light
I looked into our child's eyes and saw an unpleasant plight
The love she was conceived with had pride and happiness
And she will be the key … to release my loneliness
I know I'm made of more! I no longer feel alone
I will learn to fight my demons, then cast them off my thrown
Oh Man, this won't be easy for the thought that you once cared
Must help separate my hatred to see the love that we once shared
Yes! I'll receive this as a lesson a gift from me to you
I will earn my Masters Degree with a change in Attitude
I will call upon my Angles, my Masters and the like
Pray that they release me with peace and then insight
It is time to show forgiveness not for you but more for me!
To bring about a change and teach all children to be free
I pray to you Dear Jesus, please help me see this through
Forgive my Roman soldiers just as you once had to do
I guess I chose this lesson. Although quite unknown it's true
If my life is to be peaceful there is one thing I must do
Release myself of loathing and extend only love to you
For if I'm to be an example I must show good morals too!

In the book "The Little Soul and the Sun," written by Neale Donald Walsch, we are reminded that God has sent us nothing but angels. If we remember this, rather than focusing on revenge and our own egotistical righteousness, we will come to the understanding that God and life are one. Only when we unconditionally accept the right of another to have a different opinion can we begin to extend that tolerance to strangers.
This is not necessarily an easy stance to take, because in doing so we will have to take responsibility for our own participation.

Keep in mind that the poor behaviors of others are merely reflections of our own mishaps, and that they have been presented to us as a reminder of what we do not want to repeat. The choice is ours as to how we're going to react. There are no mistakes in life, only lessons. If we don't choose to learn from the lessons being presented, we can pretty much bank on having them presented again, either in the form of another love relationship, business relationship, or addiction. No matter how much we complain about a difficult situation, if we sit back and reflect on exactly how it came about, we will undoubtedly recognize our role in its creation.

Our growth is a process of trials and errors. Have you ever watched a child who is learning to walk? She gets up, falls down, gets up, falls down, gets up again and perhaps falls down again, or she takes off running. But the child doesn't give up. Only when we become adults do we learn about failure and giving up. Our learning never ends, but we will never learn if we continue to point blame at others and fail to take ownership of what is ours. So often we get stuck, not only in the box, but packed in the corner like sardines in a can. We become hard and fixed on one way of thinking, not willing to open up to any attempts offered by others to help us release. Instead, we reject others, and rather than accepting a helping hand, we view it as slap on the face. All gifts fall on deaf ears, and we continue to repeat our past mistakes crying, "Woe is me!" or "If I had the breaks you had, I could be successful too."

We come into this world in a suit with no pockets, and we leave wearing the same suit. What we choose to pick up along the way and how we choose to handle it will make the difference in the end result. If we make different choices than those of our parents, our lives will become free of their addictions and prejudice.

"The beginning of knowledge is the discovery of something we do not understand."
– Frank Herbert

Just like Daddy

When I was very little and you were very young
I really loved you Daddy you were number one
All I saw was good in you and faults. Well you had none!
And when I needed help I knew that you would come
Soon I started growing, and school you took me there
Fear it never came to me because I knew you cared
You helped me do my homework but soon I was so smart
I started seeing boys I broke most every heart
You started disappearing and then one fateful day
You packed up all your things and moved so far away
I didn't understand what happened to our home?
I thought that we were happy but, Mom was all alone
I denied your imperfections for all too many years
Ignored all your addictions and then all Mommy's tears
I sought my isolation as a safe place for me to run
In there was a world of fantasy and a *Princess* I'd become
I soon met my *Prince Charming,* he looked a lot like you
Again there was no detection of faults for me to view
One day I thought we'd marry and have a child or two
But him, he feared commitment. Oh, yes a lot like you!
Now I have a daughter and I'm alone here too
I think I've learned a lesson I'll share with both of you
If you love your Daddy make sure you see him through
A pair a real clear glasses, the rose colored cloud your view
There is a happy ending to this story I must say
Dad's third wife saw him coming and knew just how to play
His game it was soon over it took patience to help him stay
It took a lot of years to finally rise above
The personal afflictions of unrequited love
And now that he is happy I see that this could be
A definite possibility for you and then there's always me
I found the door to happiness and forgiveness was the key!

Help

I asked you for your help … but that you could not give
You offered me some guidance and prayer to help me live
I've had my share of troubles of which I did create
For years I blamed most other using lust to help sedate
I was living in my past and feeding it with hate
I brought it to my present and couldn't see it was to late
I put it in a special place to compromise my pride
I made up the excuses and managed to just hide
And as the rules got harder I blamed others for my stay
When bad days would befall me … I tried so hard to run away
Looking for the cure … I lived for my tomorrow
Thinking I could hide away the fear of selfish horror
Yes, portions of my traumas were clearly served by others
But it's I that must release them to clean my soiled covers
I hung around with … *Asses* ... adding insult to my grief
I wallowed in my anger and fed my addictions for relief
This soon became my illness as I fed it everyday
I lied to friends and family … and soon they went away
I thought I had some freedom, power and control
I lost my sense of honor … I fell into a hole
I see your helping hand as a life line and pray it will remain
I beg you *Spirit* guide me … to a quiet peaceful plain …

Joanna and James were married in the late 1960s. Joanna stayed home with the children while James worked two jobs to make ends meet. This worked out fine while the children were growing up, but once they moved out, Joanna became house bound. She suffered from depression and a dose of empty nest syndrome. She decided to go back to school to pursue her teaching degree. This seemed like a good idea at first, but eventually James felt that he was being neglected. Some of Joanna's classes were in the evening. This did not sit well with James, for he had a pattern of expecting his dinner on the table as soon as he got home, and now this was no longer the case. Joanna did have his dinner in the microwave, but this was not enough.

James, not wanting to look as though he were holding Joanna back from her new career, started to complain, using sarcastic innuendos about her extra curricular activities. By the end of the first semester, James was airing his grievances in a very nasty fashion to whoever would listen. His intention was to intimidate Joanna enough to force her to give up her dream. When she brought home a study partner, James would use inappropriate language and sarcasm, making it extremely uncomfortable. Soon Joanna became totally disgusted with Jim's behavior, and opted to do her work at the library.

James refused to recognize his arrogance, so eventually the couple separated. James became increasingly agitated at his wife's decision to remove herself from the stress. One evening after a night out with the boys, James went to Joanna's apartment. He tried at first to reason with Joanna. When he realized that Joanna was not buying it, he got louder, and then he became violent. Joanna had to have him physically removed from her apartment.

James was ordered by the court to take anger management classes for ten months. After eight months, James finally had his "Ah ha!" moment. He had a breakthrough that forced him to admit to his stubbornness, but he was far from total recovery. He knew if he didn't make a permanent change in his behavior, there was a good chance that he would end up alone, watching television with nothing but his ego and a channel changer. He agreed to go to couple's counseling.

However, James was not completely ready to take responsibility for his actions, until he realized that Joanna was not coming back into the relationship unless he got serious. It was at this point that he knew he had to make a choice between his pride and his happiness.

James was forced to recognize that through his fear of losing Joanna, he had been sabotaging not only his relationship with her, but also any success in his career. He was manifesting what he feared most.

"Any fool can criticize condemn and complain – and most fools do" –*Dale Carnegie*

Deception

I've been *deceived* by my perceptions for all to many years
I felt I was the only one that had no apparent fears
I saw the faults of others and failed to understand
My view was one of *selfishness* I was stubborn but in command!

When others tried to warn me of the arrogance in my tone
I boosted and got louder as though I were royalty on a throne
The people I attracted I thought admired me
I couldn't understand why they seemed so tired of me

My friends all seemed so phony no substance did they have
They always wanted something to benefit their craft
I felt my life was lacking I had no quality you see
Perhaps my lack of *integrity* was catching up with me

There was a change that I was seeking but I didn't have a clue
I didn't even recognize the love I had for you
The times you tried to tell me I let your words just pass
By making you feel stupid God, I was such as ass

Today I am real sorry and I do *apologize*
For if I hadn't been so full of Me
We could have shared our lives
My life I will be changing I'm no one to *Criticize!*

Last year my husband and I went to Vancouver, Canada on vacation. Flying is not one of my favorite means of travel, especially under the circumstances today: the terrorist alerts, delayed flights, baggage searches, and all the other hassles that accompany even the most routine of flights. On this particular trip, we also had to contend with customs. I usually keep myself entertained by reading a book, but for some reason I misplaced my book, so I decided to do some people watching. The crowded corridors were filled with people of all ages, races, genders and nationalities, all scurrying about their business. It was no great surprise to see the people in the airport focusing on their gate number, flight time, location of their baggage, packet of tickets, children, and all the other things one needs to pay attention to when traveling.

However, once we were boarded and settled into our seats, I thought things would settle down. But things did not calm down; discord was the theme.

Couples were complaining about the traffic on the way to the airport, young children were crying, a few elderly people looked distressed, as though they had little experience in air travel. Even the people with window seats were either sleeping or having some sort of exchange with the person seated beside them. Much to my dismay, I noticed that there were not many smiles. We were flying over the mountains, lakes, and beautiful land of the northern Rocky Mountains, yet no one seemed to care.

I was fortunate enough to have a window seat. I couldn't take my eyes off of the majestic beauty of the vast landscape, with its frozen lakes and snow covered mountain tops. Occasionally, I would notice an animal foraging for food, or perhaps just enjoying the beauty of its natural home. My husband and I shared this view, feeling in awe of its quiet, untouched beauty. Suddenly, the flight attendant interrupted, offering a stale bag of crackers and a soda. At that point, my window gazing was interrupted by the person in front of me who decided that it was time for a nap. He reclined his seat as far as he could, not noticing or caring that the only thing separating his head from my lap was a thin piece of plastic and foam rubber. I tapped him on the shoulder and politely asked if he would mind just raising his seat a bit, because my knees were pinned by the back of it.

He snapped at me saying, "I paid for my seat, lady. If you wanted room, you should have gone first class."

All righty, then! I decided he must have been one of the guys fighting traffic on the way to the airport.

His partner blurted out, "Do you have to be so rude all the time?"

They bantered back and forth for several minutes, until the flight attendant interrupted, offering another selection of snacks and candy bars along with a selection of coffee, tea or soda pop.

I soon noticed that the mood was not isolated to this one couple. It seemed that almost everyone on the flight was so self absorbed that they were failing to enjoy the simplest of pleasures.

When we arrived in Vancouver, I observed that the mood in the airport was quite different. The majority of the people were either Oriental or West Indian, and they were calm and untouched by the massive confusion of the arriving and departing flights. My husband flagged down a porter, and together they loaded our bags onto a cart. I noticed a significant difference in the behaviors of the Yuppies between the ages of 25 and 45, and that of the over 50 crowd. Apparently, so did the porters, for while the younger groups were scrambling and snapping at each other to grab a porter, I noticed the porters were not necessarily ignoring the Yuppies, but they tended to the older folks first. I also noticed the younger men barking at their female companions to get this or hold that, while the young ladies were intently studying the competition. The whole scene was like something out of Twilight Zone.

As the trip progressed, it became more apparent that the Yuppies were not interested in the beauty of the mountains or lakes. They were more interested in which bar or mall they should go to first. The teenagers complained about how bored they were, and the parents complained about how expensive everything was.

My husband played golf while I sat on the balcony, enjoying my book and the cool mountain air. Coming from hot and humid Florida, this was a refreshing change. Later that evening we joined a few of the couples from our group for dinner, which was followed by drinks at a comedy club. The Yuppies were buying rounds of drinks as though the night would never end. Not being drinkers, my husband and I decided to walk back to the hotel. It was wonderful! The sky was a deep blue-black, sprinkled with gem like stars of all sizes and depths. It was as though you were looking into infinity.

My heart was bursting with a feeling of appreciation for this awesome beauty. As we walked back to our hotel, we were approached by a pan handler adorned in scruffy clothing and a broad toothless smile. My husband reached into his pocket and handed him a ten dollar bill and some loose change. You would've thought that he'd just hit the lottery. The man took my husband's hand in his and with soulful eyes, thanked him and then proceeded to point out the beautiful night lights in the sky.

He said, "Welcome to my living room."

This was a person living on the streets with no roof over his head or comfortable bed to sleep in, and he was in love with the living room provided by Mother Nature. I was thinking about the atmosphere during our arrival into Canada; the sophisticated people who found pleasure in poking fun at the weaknesses and disadvantages of others. I wondered, if they were to meet a stranger in their hometown, would they be as hospitable? Furthermore, would they have even noticed the vast jewel like mural painted on their ceiling?

"Think about the beauty still left around you and be happy"
—Anne Frank

Mountains

I flew above the Mountains and soared between the clouds
I saw the Lakes and Oceans and fields that farmers plowed
As, I marveled at their Majesty and the awesome view
I did begin to wonder? Why so much attitude?
I watched as people spoke most conversations lame
They had no real importance mostly anger and misled Blame
Why not appreciate these gifts God gave us in his name?
Instead we spread resentment and pass it on with Shame

Have we become so shallow our calluses so thick?
That we don't see or recognize that this is just a trick
It is "Ego's" vicious madness a narcissistic game
One if we continue will ruin us the same …
Lost like Ancient Empires and Dynasties that failed
Perhaps we should see history and shed the pain we veiled
The times need to be changing our youth is proof of that
Just watch them as their taking from where ever they are at

What has happened to our cultures that we've become so blind
We have spared the rod and discipline …
Afraid to leave a friend behind so now we've created monsters
With, shallow points of view and wonder why their rotten
Perhaps, it is what we do it's spreading like a wild fire
Scorching all who tread the path …
Our selfishness is destroying us it is time to do the math!
Collectively, we created it. Now, it must be undone
For if we do not change it World Peace there will be *None!*

Ego Feeding Anger

EGO suckles on your soul as if an infant starving
It plays with you so you can view how it can be alarming!
Anger, joins its mighty force and soon will come the shame
It seems to me that it should be with pride and senseless fame
Right or wrong it will not care Ego tells me that!
It does just what it wants to do it like a tenacious cat!
Consequence! There will be none. For your Ego will not pay
This world is yours to take not share Ego serves you everyday!
But, soon in time I hope you'll see the price you'll have to pay
Declaring me with no integrity it is time I walk away!
You sucked me dry my tears are gone you took all I could give
I'm tired now it doesn't matter indifference is where I live!
The love I had has all gone bad because it had no honor!
I scream out loud *"I Hope Your Proud!"*
For now you are alone!
Is this the life you want to live a prisoner to your anger?
That's not the way life has to be the bars and walls can crumble
For when ego dies the soul revives …
As life becomes quite humble
Humility and honesty are stepping stones at least!
They'll feed us growth with integrity
And grant us lasting peace!
Give ego up it serves no man least not where truth resides
For Ego is a place to hide ones adolescent pride
An entity that uses fear and arrogance for strength
It hides behind the shameful lies masked by pure contempt
Once released the soul is free when Ego has moved on
Your life will be with *harmony* and your soul will be *Reborn!*

When Elizabeth came to me, she was suffering from depression and rage. She and her partner of 12 years had recently had a baby. Although she knew he wasn't crazy about the idea of having a family, she thought that once the baby arrived, he would come around. Unfortunately, he didn't, for approximately 6 months after the baby was born her partner announced that he could not continue with the relationship and felt that it was in their best interest to separate. She was devastated and confused, not knowing which way was up. She lost weight, cried herself to sleep, blamed herself for the failed relationship, and allowed her self esteem to hit an all time low.

For the next 12 months, she experienced mixed feelings of depression, abandonment, denial, confusion, rage, indifference, and finally, acceptance. These same feelings often occur after a sudden death or divorce, or even a break up in a business partnership. Frequently, we are so involved in our fantasies of how a relationship should be that we fail to pay attention to the signs of an impending failure, and when it happens we feel as though we had been put on an iceberg in the Caribbean.

We tend to go into a mode of denial, grasping for excuses and often plotting revenge or retribution. Our friends and family could sympathize with us until chickens grew lips, but the bottom line is, if we don't see our part in the break-up, words of wisdom will have no meaning. Separations are never easy, even under the best of circumstances. All too often, well meaning family members and friends are more than willing to take sides, adding insult to injury. It would be wise to stay as neutral as possible, because only the two people involved in the relationship know what was said behind closed doors.

Understanding the magnitude of someone else's pain is never easy, and staying unbiased is even more difficult. One needs to listen between the lines of rejection, and guide the injured party to identify their role in the separation. Soul searching is never easy, especially when harsh words were exchanged out of anger, and delicate egos have been bruised. It is important to get past the ego and to recognize the reality of what happened. By examining your fears with naked honesty, you will come to the truth. By surrendering ego's demands and re-evaluating your position, you will most likely understand that, as painful as it may seem at the time, there is a valuable lesson to be learned. This is a time to weigh out your emotions, then ask yourself, "Is this what I need, or what I want?" Your wants will always be greater than your needs, but your needs will always serve your highest purpose.

Your lesson is to accept the challenge, and perhaps you will find that by serving your needs now, your wants will bring in even greater abundance in the future. When you need someone to talk to (and you will), find someone who will tell you what you need to hear, not want you want to hear. The only way you will get any clarity is with the truth, and the truth is not always the easiest path. While this is a difficult time, it is also a crossroad to your future, and given time it will pass. Remember that no matter what the outcome, neither party is the bad guy. Things are just changing because growth is needed. Ask God for the guidance to make the right choices and the insight to see the higher path through selflessness. All roads lead to peace. **E**dging **G**od **O**ut is an off ramp to nowhere.

The following story poems are a reflection of the feelings that couples experience from the beginning of a break up, through the healing process and beyond. It was my intention not to take sides but to point out that when sides are taken, hurt becomes the master and no one wins. Often we allow our assumptions to rule our behavior, and grave mistakes come from what at the time seemed to be good choices.

Healing takes time, and if it is done with authenticity we will most likely come to realize that no one person was at fault. Communication, or shall I say, a lack of communication, is the major component for most failed relationships. When expectations are not shared or discussed, they will likely go belly up because of one or both parties fear of rejection or losing control. Their individual wants or needs become the main focus, resulting in the manifestation of their greatest fear.

"The greatest discovery of my generation is that a human being can alter his life by altering his attitude of mind."
—William James

Right Between the Eyes

You hit me with *confusion* right between the Eyes!
Perhaps, with all the quarreling …
I should not have been *Surprised*
I knew our points of view were often not the same
Being from different cultures made for an interesting game
I thought we'd overcome it …
And our love would guide us through
I guess that I was wrong but, then you already knew
Our elders they did warn us with what they wanted us to do
They kept us close to family and in our own neighborhood too
It was to our Misfortune for what we could NOT see …
Was if we'd stayed in our commitment our love it still might be
We gave in to the pressures and as stubborn as could be
We put the hurt inside us and stored it *Personally*
The words that were directed were meant to cut right through
Sharper than a sword the Samurai once threw
That day you took a part of me it damaged me for life
Some say to just forget it discard it and let it go
But in my heart I'm bleeding I can't help but let it show
I know that time will heal me and one night I might sleep
For now I'm in depression it pulls me down so deep
I fight from feeling weary but it's hard as it can be
Everywhere I look I see pictures of you with me
I'm as weak as a young fledgling that's fallen from a tree
My judgment comes so quickly I can't focus nor can I see
The world is spinning rapidly despite my energy
I can't allow this *bitterness* to take a hold of me
My friends say I should hate you for what you've done to me
You know what? I can't do that for when I look at you I see
The vulnerable little boy … that you were never allowed too be

Pedestal

I put you on a pedestal I thought you were a *God*
You put me on a shelf at the time it seemed quite odd
I watched you as you grew perfection was your Goal
Selfishness and vanity these culprits took your Soul
As time went on I could not see my love was blinding me
I worshipped every step you took I thought you were so smart
But it seems that your *deception* was your overwhelming art

Right now it seems you're happy and this is good for you
As for me, my spirits broken my heart is wounded too
I guess I should be bitter? But, I won't waste time on you
I'll pray for some protection and ask God that I be *healed*
Soon I will recover and gain the power I once concealed
The pleasures you have now are worth but one small dime
I thought that I once knew you perhaps that was my crime

You sold me out for passion and, flesh that's what I'm told
Now let me ask you this? How could you've been so cold?
I pose to you this question don't tell me it's not true
Why did you hurt your family we're flesh and blood to you!
Did you not think we mattered? Or did you just not care?
Or were we of lesser value …
Then your tawdry, cheap, affair?

A Different Point of View

You put me on a Pedestal this made life hard for me
You *expected* the perfection of one I could not be
I tired so hard to love you and be a family
But, fear of this commitment scared the living *Hell* from me!
There were times I tired to tell you perhaps we didn't share
Our emotions were well hidden it was fear that kept them there
In my heart I am so puzzled confused and sometimes blind!
I think I know what I want and then, I change my mind
I never meant to hurt you … I know you won't believe
My lies they were discovered and rightfully you're *peeved!*
I've done things I'm not proud of that you can be sure
One thing I'm truly sure of … *mistakes* I will make more!
I'm not of shear perfection I'm sure you will agree
I fall into temptation it is the faulty part of me!
One day I might/could change this when this day does come
I hope that you'll forgive me for being such a crumb
I wanted to protect you from thoughts deep in my past
When it comes down to commitments I fear they'll never last
This fear is mine alone with prayer I'll learn to cope
Until that day arrives I keep looking for some hope
Your life it needs commitment and I will not lie to you
I doubt that I can do the things you want me to
The things that you deserve won't keep me loving you
These things I can not promise for they are not a part of me
By now you are probably thinking …
"How shallow can he be?"

Perhaps, you are correct and it's time for *honesty*
I don't know how to change it … Or if I want to try?
Because the way I see it, I'm just another Guy!
I'm sure they'll come a day when I will finally see
The pride and pleasures that I took were only serving me
But you … You need security I'm afraid I can't provide
So for now you must go forward without me by your side
I pray that you'll forgive me for the pain that I have caused
If it's any consolation I hope that you will see …
The fall from that great pedestal is also hurting ME!

Temptress

You *thought* I was your lover, your whore, your concubine!
You *chose* me over another we had no boundaries at the time
I will treat you as a *King* now and lavish you with tricks!
But! Once it is all over you'll know it was for *kicks!*
Your feelings they won't matter for once I'm used to you
I will throw you to the side like a tattered leather shoe …

You will want my full commitment but that I can *not* do!
Because then I will remember the one you over through!
If you could do that to her and your child too
Then I would be a *Fool!* Not to see through you
You are a game to me one, I can put away
And then take out to play on any given day!

I have you by the Heart and your short hairs too
I will *chew* you up in pieces then spit you out of view
You may come back for more of what I give to you
But, remember I'm like a *viper* waiting in the night
So if you're not around I'll find someone else to bite!
I may enjoy a morsel and take a taste or two …

But do *not* depend on me I'll *never* cherish you!
Don't think that you can trust me this I'm telling you!
When it comes to loving life there is only one in my view
For I am independent a person of great means
There is no other shoulder upon which I need to lean!
This may seem very selfish and a tad bit callous to …

But, I am a survivor *not* looking out for you!
So take a second look of what you had to do
And ask if it was worth it for I will *demolish* you
I will feed you your addiction and play your porno too
Remember when it's over what a *Rattle Snake* can do
Your flesh may feel some pleasure but I will *kill* your brain!

There will be no pleasant memories only one's of *pain!*
So this advice I'll give you accept all words of prayer
Being said for you by family and friends that really care!
Ask God to take your fear and your addictions too
Then put them in his hands for you will find that once you do
I will be long gone and true *freedom* will come to you!

Across the Table

We sit across the table and though we're face to face!
For as much as we *communicate!* We could be in a different place
Our love was made of passion …
For Oh, so many years we hid behind our bodies
And never shared our fears!
Our goals they were so different, but how were we to know?
We based our whole relationship
On what was A *Broadway Show*…
When we were presented with a whole new way of life
You feared that we might separate …
If you could not control my life!
We tried hard to avoid it but still it had to come
I suffered devastation and thought that you had none
Again we weren't seeing the things we did create
Being *Right!* Was more important then trying to relate
I guess this was a lesson we both needed to discern
Thoughts are things, we manifest I hope they'll help us learn!
And now, as time is passing I hope we can sedate
All these righteous feelings that won't allow us to relate!
Slowly, we are learning to share our guarded fears
You know the one's we hid inside for all too many years
We thought this was a bad thing but, we're about to learn
When *Spirit* grants our wishes…
We must think with some concern!
Be mindful of what is asked for and make it very clear
At this time we should separate the passion from the fear
Well, now I'm here to tell you from this lesson I have learned
For my mindset it has changed and happiness I've earned
Next time I cross that table I will communicate!
There will be no more hiding from which I can't relate
I will find it through good counsel good books and honesty
I will educate myself and teach myself to be
A happy open person with a Spirit that is *Free!*

New relationships are such an adventure. We walk around holding in our stomachs, breathing into our hands to check our breath, carefully choosing our food in their presence. Men like to make sure that they are clean shaven and groomed, and women prep and primp so each hair is carefully sitting in the right position. Conversations are seldom candid, and are often exaggerated stories that were rehearsed the night before. Our hormones are on high alert, as their alluring perfumes permeate the atmosphere. We are pursuers of love and lust, reeling in our prey, only to toy with the vulnerable and throw back the rest.

Our society has indulged this great hunt, and even provided workshops in the form of reality shows on television, dating services, and newspaper advertisements. There is the worldwide web on the Internet and clubs introducing men to women, men to men, and women to women. Photos are provided along with personal profiles, the likes and dislikes, even right down to the color of one's eyes. We have become so high tech that we are losing sight of really getting to know a person. Rather than having a conversation, we immediately indulge in copulation. Then when the fantasy becomes a reality, we discover the burps and farts, bad breath and bed heads.

Dreams of commitment become nightmares of reality. Then one morning you wake up, and Prince Charming or Sleeping Beauty has been transformed into a mythical beast and bitch. Or have they? Perhaps the myth was that of Prince Charming and Sleeping Beauty, and the reality was the other. In my opinion, relationships have assumed the hectic pace of get it done and run along with the rest of society. People don't take the time to get to know one another. Instead, the general consensus is that if it feels good, do it, and if it looks good, buy it.

To paraphrase one of my students when she was asked how she was going to work out a problem, she replied, "No worries." This could be the case if society was trained to go with the flow, but as a rule it is not.

Once the initial physical interaction is carried out, a feeling of possession overrides our common sense and the little white lies conscience. If not behaving with total honesty, we begin to have doubts about our worthiness. Then the all too familiar feelings of guilt, fear, blame or shame override intuitive gut feelings, and we are right back where we started, participating in another shallow relationship, making excuses for dishonorable behaviors by using little white lies.

We all have a story. The question is, can we step out of our fantasies long enough to be honest about our vulnerability? Can we enter into a lasting relationship, baring our souls rather than our bottoms? I have clients, both men and women, who come in complaining about their significant other, only to find that when the relationship began, both parties entered into it as though they were attending a masquerade ball – not acknowledging their own insecurities, pretending to have control over their emotions, and avoiding any exposure to their weaknesses. How can anyone expect a relationship to last when its foundation is built on deception? Juliann is an attractive young woman in her late 20s. After receiving her college degree she started her own business doing property investments. Then she met Mark, a good looking, successful businessman who owned several businesses with offices throughout the country. They dated for approximately six months when she discovered that the man of her dreams turned out to be a nightmare. Like so many young woman today, she got wrapped up in a whirlwind relationship full of passion and promises, only to have them dashed when she accidentally caught her lover with another woman.

Although the relationship was barely out of the hand holding stage, Juliann felt sure that Mark was her Mr. Right. She was ready to make a huge commitment. Mark talked Juliann into setting up her office in his building, so they could be close. He even made suggestions about making her a part of his business investments. As soon as Mark felt he had Juliann convinced that his intentions were honorable, he started to disappear for a couple of days during the week and then on a few weekends. One Friday afternoon, Mark and Juliann were in the office. Mark's cell phone rang and he dashed toward it as if to stop Juliann from picking it up. Thinking his behavior bizarre, she asked him to tell her what was going on.

Later that evening, the phone rang again. Mark picked it up and went off into a corner, as if he had a big secret. When Juliann asked if everything was all right, he snapped at her, telling her to mind her own business. Needless to say, his response was quite troublesome. She could think of no apparent reason for his nasty reaction. That weekend there were several more calls, resulting in the same reaction. She soon became suspicious, so while Mark was sleeping she retrieved the number off his phone.

Later that week, she called the number and a woman answered. After a few pointed questions, she discovered that Mark was seeing a woman in another state who was also under the impression that she was his number one girl.

When Juliann confronted Mark about the other woman, he denied it at first. Then he said the woman was his ex-girlfriend who wanted to get back with him, but he wanted no part of her. Upon further investigation, Juliann found that Mark's story was nothing but lies. She was both crushed and embarrassed. She chastised herself for being so foolish to believe that Mark would want to bring her into his business and make her a partner after only knowing her for a few months.

Our world is so fast paced that people enter into relationships as though they were at a drive-in window of a fast food restaurant. Honesty is seldom considered, and often not even addressed until the couples are either in so deep that they fear a break-up or they leave what might have been a solid relationship, simply because they have no clue how to communicate. Both parties usually walk away, blaming each other for their miserable failures and suffering from bouts of depression and self reprisal. Perhaps, it's time to slow down.

"The truth that makes men free is for the most part the truth which men prefer not to hear." —*Herbert Agar*

Lies

Your lies they were so many I had to stop the counting
At first they were not meant to hurt …
But continued and kept mounting …
You tell me what I want to hear not what I need to know

Your flowery descriptions of how our life will grow
It is through all these deceptions that things will fall apart
But truth no matter what reception will keep us strong at heart
You think you are the Master in this sultry game

But look again my friend it's messing up your name
The wool is over *your* eyes for those around you see
Your lies and your deception are merely just a Plea
I look into your eyes and find there just a Sea

Of very lame excuses all hiding, inadequately
You can lie to others and you can lie to me
But look into the mirror as you will plainly see
These lies they are destroying you and alienating me

The truth if it be known and I hope that your will see
It is time for you right now! *"To respond with ability"*
So the next time you go shopping this isle won't be closed
The truth will be so plain to see it will sit right on your nose!

You will experience a cleansing a purging of a sort
It will make you free to practice when you used to just retort
You will find a pleasant feeling not to argue or complain
For when you tell the truth you have nothing to *Explain!*

Powwow

I tried to have a Powwow to communicate my thoughts
I had hoped that you would listen but in vanity you're lost
You say you'll show devotion and make an honest change
But then I catch you in a lie and we're back on the same page
As I look into your mirror I don't like what I see
For your still a selfish liar who is always blaming me
I prayed for you this morning and will again tonight
If you don't control your Ego your future won't be bright
Right now you can not see it but I hope in time you'll change
And once that this shift happens you'll play a whole new game
Horizons will be brightened and with clarity you'll view
You'll see that all your loneliness is what you brought to you
You mocked all those before you, thinking they were weak
But you'll find a great reward when the truth is what you speak
Now this may not come easy this change in attitude
You'll find the more you practice …
It will be received with gratitude
At first you might feel different but soon it will be old hat
You'll find that showing kindness is always where you're at
For slowly you will notice at least that's what I'm told
When you give openly to others your soul will not be sold
So start right now to practice the best that you can be
And Spirit will reward you with much tranquility
For this is the sweet bounty that we can all count on
When we show our *selflessness* we bid our *Ego* gone

For the past fifty years or so, our communities have engaged in an aggressive war against drug dealers, sexual offenders, homosexuals, and anyone else who might be considered a deviant. But there has been little progress.

When Susan was a teenager, she was sexually abused by her boyfriend's uncle, and also by a neighbor. She was so ashamed and embarrassed that she never told a soul about the uncle. However, she did tell a family member about the neighbor, only to be dismissed with the explanation that she must have been mistaken. She felt rejected, dishonored, and helpless. She felt there was little more she could do, after all, the neighbor was a professor at the local college and a pillar of the community, and the uncle was a member of her boyfriend's family. So she held her tongue and made a point of not being around either of the men.

For years she felt that she had to put up a front of being a tough girl. She used foul language, smoked cigarettes, drank with the guys, and was willing to take on anyone who challenged her. She gained the reputation of being someone you would not mess with, but her damaged soul was pleading for justice. She married at a young age, and though she loved her husband, in her heart she knew her marriage was a refuge from the real world. It was safe. Realizing that she could never change the past, she decided to make the best of the present. She settled into family life, raised her children, and quietly wrestled with her inner demons. Never feeling that she was quite good enough, she pursued her education at home by devouring every book on self-help. Though her healing process took several years, she eventually realized that if she didn't release her anger it would definitely eat a hole right through her soul.

She discovered that forgiveness had a far better reward then revenge. If she encountered someone who attempted to use verbal assaults, she would remove herself immediately. More importantly, she didn't take their ignorance as a personal affront. Instead, she would privately send them love, knowing their attacks were only a defense for the sins that had been committed against them. She developed a personal armor and systematically forgave everyone she felt had dishonored her. Those who were close to her felt she was making excuses, but in truth she just didn't see any benefit in inflicting more pain. Even if she did go through the system and social justice was served, she couldn't change the tragic events of her past and didn't want to start the nightmares all over again. Going through such personal humiliation for so long was quite enough. It was time to let go.

She decided to channel her anger in a positive direction by teaching and conducting seminars to help others who suffered from bruised and battered self-esteem. She is my friend, and I love her.

"You have power over your mind – not outside events. Realize this, and you will find strength." Marcus Aurelius

As it is

Life … is as it is
Not as it … *should* be
If it's not to you're satisfaction
You can change the things you see

Perhaps … not all the actions
Are up to … you or me
So take it as it comes
And deal with it or be

Confused … or maybe happy
It makes … no difference to me
The point is that it's happened
And there are no real mistakes

Life … is just like fishing
With flies … on mountain lakes
So release yourself of judgment
That's all it really takes

Sexual addiction is possibly one of the most misunderstood of all addictions. It will supply a sense of euphoria, but unlike other addictions you can't get away from it. The mixed messages and double standards are easily justified, depending on cultural and/or religious teachings. If you were from a native tribe in the jungles of Africa or Indonesia or another primitive country, it might be quite acceptable to indulge in masturbation or perhaps take an unmarried virgin who has just entered into puberty as your concubine, or perhaps even have multiple partners. All would be copasetic according to the accepted cultures of the land. However, in what we consider the civilized cultures, these actions would be punishable by law and the consequences would be severe.

Another misconception is that if one is pleasing him or herself with their God given equipment, then they are immediately doomed to hell. When who are they hurting, no one, actually. After all, if God didn't want you to use this gift then why did he make it feel so good? Unfortunately, like most good things there is always someone who will misunderstand its use and over indulge. Soon, they find its pleasure consuming their every thought. At that time they move their sights to a variety of sources. Alas, an addiction is born and the addict begins to prey on innocent and vulnerable victims. They soon find that the habit is damaging not only to themselves, but to others as well, even if the addicts limit themselves to a personal party using porno or sex toys as their prompters. The addicts soon become overwhelmed with feelings of shame that degrade and demoralize their self esteem. Another all too true reality is that others are being affected. After all; someone had to pose for the pictures. Most likely, the participants were not willing at first and eventually became enticed, either by the financial gratification, or their own physical addiction.

As with most addictions, the addict will justify their feelings by protecting themselves in a cocoon of denial. And if the addiction is not satisfied, they often become argumentative, controlling, and sometimes violent. But they almost always find someone else to blame for not satisfying their primal *want.*

I say "want" because addictions are behaviors that serve a person's wanted feelings not their needed feelings. This is the reason I feel education is needed far more than punishment. Granted, for the safety of the innocent, incarceration in some cases may be required, but most assuredly it should be accompanied by education. Perhaps if society would focus on the families and their basic structures there might be fewer tendencies toward these deviant behaviors: by making it mandatory to attend couple's classes before marriage licenses are issued, or once a pregnancy is revealed to a physician it would be a requirement to attend parenting classes before the child is born. This process of change would admittedly be a slow one and more than likely quite costly, but so are the welfare and addiction rehabilitation programs, which for the most part are not very effective.

Arthur was a good man with a kind and gentle spirit. He came to me because he was unable to control his anger. He went through the classes in private sessions because he didn't want his family or friends to know. He revealed that he was using his anger as a crutch to conceal his feelings of guilt for things that had happened to him when he was a teen. He had been approached by an older neighborhood boy to engage in oral sex with him, and through his curiosity he complied. His guilt was so overwhelming that he began to use marijuana. His grades in school were normally A's and B's, but dropped to low C's and F's. He made it through the eighth grade before he quit. At age 30, he was a mess, not knowing if he really wanted to live or die. He had been holding onto this guilt for nearly 15 years. When he released it, he was able to carry on with a normal married life.

Our society and religious factions are so concerned about the spread of smut that we're not focusing on normal family interactions and human reactions. Parents are afraid to hug their children or show any sort of affection in public or at home because they fear legal reprisal. Normal adolescent discovery is labeled as sexual abuse, and Big Brother is all too ready to step in with law suites or criminal actions. Yet, if these normal feelings of affection were not labeled as dirty and sinful, we very likely would not have the epidemic of sexual deviation we have today.

Just saying "no" is not enough. We have a moral obligation to say no and explain why. This will promote change. I don't know a person alive who doesn't resent another person who tries to force their values on them. However, if values and respect are taught as an option rather than a coercive book of rules, one is more likely to recognize and accept the results as positive motivators toward understanding and educating, rather than judgment and punishment.

"Freedom is forgiveness" –Rev. Diane Ackerman

Uncle Jack

Uncle Jack was out of whack with his boisterous acts of fame
For those who viewed his attitude would never see his shame
He was love and lots of fun and gave it all so free
He had a rapport of an Ambassador …
But, his hands were all over me!

I pushed away and cried one day I know that this can't be!
Is there a way for you to see? That this is hurting me
You laughed I cried and I almost died …
For what your sins had done I took your blame
And held my shame concealed from everyone

And when I told, it was *my* heart they sold
To save the Family! It was a joke that fatal stroke
That brushed the private part of me …
So, many years he stood revered adding insult to injury
And now I see that part of me that honors who *"I am"*

You were a beast and an awful ghoul …
Whose life was just a Sham! So now you're gone
And that's Ok … In fact it's fine with me
I've licked my wounds and healed my Soul
And strong I am today I took your space and in its place

I put respect you see! Now it's not too late
To educate a naive society for then we'll be with boundary
And a "healthy" family! Sins of the past will only last
If we accept them as … Ok! So if you start your crap today
This game we will not play…We will correct you …

And then reject you and have you put away!

Depression

Sometimes I'm so *depressed* that all I do is cry
I wonder, is life worth it or should I allow myself to die?
I've been to all the meetings and heard the reasons why
They say that life is worth it. Please, *God* assure me you don't lie
Some say I have a purpose of which I have no clue
It seems the more I care the less that others do
My heart it feels so empty my brain just might explode
My thoughts they never stop there every where I go
My children will forsake me and my spouse I hardly know
We have created such a distance we no longer seem to flow
Yet, I do still love him and pray it's not too late
His Ego has consumed him with selfishness and hate

At times his light will flicker I see the man I miss
I long for his gentle touch and then a loving kiss
It's those moments that I yearn for the times we were alone
No selfish interruptions no food and no cell phone
He sees me as a victim one who will just cry
He feeds me his depression as he continues with his lie
He hides beneath the layers that his *Ego* did create
I guess this is my purpose to be open and communicate
So now I beg you *Spirit* please banish all the rules
Shroud me with your likeness and provide me with the tools
My strength it is well hidden but, I know that it exists
I will wield the sword of Michael and rejection I'll resist

I feel God's flame inside me I know I must persist
Just grant me the forgiveness when all I feel is pissed.
I'll turn the other cheek and look the other way
For I know that with your guidance love will come to stay
Perhaps this is my purpose going hand in hand with you
As we clear this path together we will help our children to
I see I do have purpose and I know I will create
A peaceful loving place with no resentment and no hate
By releasing my depression and putting pity out of view
I'll no longer feed the gossip my facts will all be true
When you start with accusations I will give you a strong clue
I'll no longer be your whipping girl *I'm getting over you!*

Rare Breed

Rare is the breed … that won't try to impede
The pursuit of success by another

For often it's found … that when *ego* is around
It is bound to destroy or just smother

Once it's *released* … and seen as the beast
Then there'll be only love for the other

So let's turn around … all the hate that is found
And send *peace* to all of our brothers

If judgments aren't past …we'll have acceptance at last
The *consequence* will be our druthers

Freewill gives us choice … to exercise our voice
And control *won't* be used as a cover

Thank You

I take this time to thank you for what you've shared with me
Your suicides, addictions and your adversity
In this time we've criticized, we've laughed, and even cried
But, all of us released our fears well hidden by foolish pride
There were times that we denied our fears
As they came rushing through …
But naked honesty is *"Not"* often a clear and vibrant view!
So now we know the difference and self pity we won't have
If we stumble on that beach front we will tread a bramble path

Our new path is acceptance and love for our… own self
By putting all our questions in the pantry on *God's* shelf
We'll starve our hungry *"Ego"* and allow ourselves to show
That if we want to change our life
We must trust the G*od* we know
We all know that it is easy to say these words real clear
But if we mean to do it we must *release* all the fear
Our fears are what we pick up on the road from birth to death
They cling to guilt and anger with fathoms of great depth

So when we look at others and see their darkest night
Remember we're all brothers …
Here to make our lights shine bright!
We must let go of our judgment and let our love shine through
For what we are revealing is that part of me and you
As we empty all our pockets our suits become so clean
That it is impossible for us to be any part of... *mean*
Forgiving we are finding is not one word but two
For it will bring a peace to me *for- giving* it to you!

Audrey's parents divorced when she was very young. Her mother was consumed with finding the right man to provide her with the highest social and financial position possible. Her father showed little or no respect for women; he dated beauty queens and strippers. Neither was particularly interested in the needs of their child. As a result, Audrey's perception of family was shallow and self centered. When she was young her father used her as a pawn to attract women, by exploiting his cute little girl as being abandoned by her birth mother. He would count on the maternal instincts of his often barren girl friends by encouraging them to bond, and sweetened the pot by providing shopping trips and weekend sleepovers. Once he made them feel secure, he would make excuses about having to attend business meetings out of town, leaving his lady friend home to baby-sit. He would then set the nets for another unsuspecting victim, knowing full well that eventually his stay at home victim would either suspect his misdeeds or Audrey would rat him out. He not only used his women friends, but his daughter as well.

Once her Mom found a stepfather who could support her lavish life style, he indulged her insecurities with numerous plastic surgeries, health spa retreats, and fad diets. There was little or no focus on her daughter's needs.

It was no wonder that Audrey had become a bitter, shallow person with no respect for relationships or marriage. She had developed a callous survival attitude, neither wanting nor needing permanence. Girlfriends were suspicious of her and her guy friends used her for one night stands and booty calls. Her biggest fear was that she would not have a boyfriend to fill in when Daddy's money ran out. While she was quite intelligent, the only talent she managed to master was her sex appeal. It had become her meal ticket.

"Confidence is the sexiest thing a woman can have. It's much sexier than any body part." *–Aimee Mullins*

Body Addiction

My body is my addiction I play with it *Everyday!*
It has no healthy purpose it falls to my own prey
It was meant to be a *"Temple"* a housing for my Soul
But, now I roughed this structure and jumped into a hole!
I hurt so many others with this *Unhealthy Habit!*
I've become a savage dog one who is almost rabid!

I know it's not for me it is not what *GOD* intended
I have a healthy mind but my thoughts have been suspended!
My pleasure started young! I trusted all my teachers
Some of them were kin and some of them were preachers!
It is hard for me to see the person I'm meant to be
But, with your guided help Oh, *Lord!* I'm sure I could be Free

I must respect my sisters, my brothers and their wives
A task I fell so short of when patronizing dives
These places were not buildings they dwelled within my head
That fantasy I made for me and then brought it to my bed!
I know this is unhealthy or that is what I'm told?
They say the Truth will free you but, I don't know if I'm sold

I look into a mirror and see there no *Respect!*
My Angel is inside me just wanting to *Reflect!*
My life will have perspective and love will soon return
When I display the peacefulness that honesty will earn
I will purchase all my actions and then apologize
For all the pain I dealt you because of all my *Lies!*

Fear

Fear it is my enemy it binds me to my rage
It plays on my emotions as though if were a plague
All that I've been taught is shadowed with great shame
The fear that haunts my being controls me with its blame

Anger is fears sister a sibling I won't see
One that creates a *Poison* that will only damage me
My teachers all have taught me to listen to their rules
To follow without question than swim in their *Cesspools!*

Pollution of my mind has corroded all that's good!
Keeping me from believing in a trusted brotherhood
It's time that I am freed from all the lies I see
And start a new beginning by trusting in my *Me!*

I know I am a wise one but I've been blinded by your might
Fear you're not my brother in spite of all your fright!
So if I'm to be honest and I'm to be free
I must release your controlling deception and mediocrity

I deny you of your pleasure and release you from command!
It is me I want to see who is now in great Demand!
My Truth is standing for me and that's been hard to see
My freewill is my leader and my choices are the key

Fear, you're not my friend now, nor something I believe!
It's taken me some eons to earn my own reprieve
I will not sit as your hostage and you're not where I'm to live
My heart has opened up now as *"Spirit"* has shown me how
I can live alone without you I'm in control and I am *Proud!*

Tunnel Vision

I woke up very late one night a panic not explained
A monster walking in my hall with huffs and bloody fangs
I cried for Mom but she was gone …
Nowhere could she be found
I cried and tired to lock the door …
My thoughts to Hell were bound …

Who was this man that wanted me?
This savage beast of schemes
He dwelled within my Soul so deep …
And tried to steal my dreams
Then I saw a Light that night …
It came to guide me with new scenes

Its embers were protecting me
From nightmares and bad dreams
Surrounding me with a blue white light …
That made me feel so safe …
I knew that with the love of *God*
No one could shake my faith!

You will question me and that's ok
Because, I will not bend …
I know that when my road is rough
The *"Holy Spirit"* is my friend!
For on that night so long ago
There was a choice I made

I may not know what is good for me
So in *God* I put my Faith
Some ask me if I believe in him
And to them I will say no …
To love my *God* I can't believe
He's someone, I must *"Know!"*

Lessons

I watched you as you suffered and took all his abuse
I didn't understand and thought *"Oh what is the use?"*
I knew I couldn't help you for I was just a kid
Although I'd run to hide I still saw what he did!
I patted all your bruises and got dark glasses for your eyes
But soon it was to late there was no more disguise!
I prayed that GOD would help you to get away right then
You had no strength to leave you were afraid of him

As I got much older I decided not to be the living punching bag
That he would beat so free … I thank you for the lesson
I learned so well from you every time he beat you
I would see your mental pain
That's when I made the choice to get you on a plane
I took you far away so you could heal and then regain
The strength and self esteem you allowed him to claim
I know that GOD was listening because just look at you!

Your radiance is showing and your eyes they twinkle too
I see it when you watch me you grin from ear to ear
There is no more expression of the anguish or the fear
Now when I have children I will know just what to do
Teach them love with confidence for themselves and others to
Make their boundaries stead fast offer them respect
Show that our anger is not something to reject
But an emotion we can direct when we properly do reflect!

Teacher

You came here as a *teacher* I learned a lot from you
Each day a new adventure and lessons to review
Some were not so easy they hurt along the way
I knew the day I met you the journey was not all play
We shared so much together our different points of view
And learned to accept each other for the best that we could do
Despite our friends and family and their opinions too
I never lost sight … of the love I have for you

There were times that you did *hurt* me
But I could see right through the past that you were holding
Was slowly eating you … we both have our green monsters
From our childhood they came …
It's time that we release them or we will do the same
Our *gift* won't be a scholarship of punishment and blame!
Our campus has green pastures with many flowers too
Perhaps we need to see them and appreciate their view

I make this *promise* to you no matter what you say
I won't put judgment to you a game I just won't play!
You have your own opinion and yes I will have mine
God gave us the freewill to *change* our paradigm
So when you tell your story I won't be listening to you
I will get my facts together before confronting too
For now I know that it's Ok …
To have a *different* point of view!

Often when couples have been together for a number of years, they find a comfort zone, but one that is not always the best place to be. The once respected boundaries wither and decay, turning into feelings of contempt and indifference. Families split apart, marriages end in divorce, and long time friends exchange verbal barbs of sarcasm and scorn. Both parties may walk away scratching their heads, thinking there will never be a peaceful solution. It is only when they give themselves the space and time to reevaluate that they recognize the value of their relationships.

We fail to see the cycles of life and often live in our past, only holding on to the good old days when everything seemed to be going our way. This is the problem. Everything was going our way, but by being so focused on our needs, we failed to see that our partner had needs as well. Co-dependency takes a front seat while addictions are fed and self-esteem is whittled to mere splinters of what used to be a mighty oak. This is not the fault of one person. It may take years of feeding inherited fears and feelings of guilt to cultivate these falling empires.

Pride, ego, and feelings of righteousness stemming from archaic belief systems handed down from cultural and religious philosophies tend to destroy the values they originally intended to hold sacred. Fear of losing control of what was once considered a comfort zone causes relationships that were held together with respect and consideration for each other to soon crumble, with neither party knowing how to reconnect. Words are repressed and replaced by humorous sarcasm. Soon, feelings of resentment and rejection take the place of what once was a willing intimacy.

The ego is triumphant as we turn our backs and walk away, to enter what may seem to be a better world. We soon find that by not dealing with selfishness, we are creating a future past. Have you ever asked yourself why you seem to attract the same type of people into your life over and over again? Perhaps this is because you've not been willing to recognize and take ownership of your piece of the puzzle. It isn't always easy for human nature to be in control. Realize that by losing control, you are creating what you fear the most. Encourage and honor another, rather than shoot esteem, but your own, as well.

"There will be a time when loud mouthed, incompetent people seem to be getting the best of you. When that happens you only have to be patient and wait for them to self destruct it never fails" –*Richard Rybolt, Author of "75 Ways to Beat Depression"*

Co-Dependency

I complained about your actions and controlling ways
They almost did destroy us for they were fed in many ways
I aided your dependency by supplying all your whims
I acted as the supplement condoning all your sins

The day that I acknowledged the damage this had done
I purchased my addiction previously thinking I had none
I posed myself some questions too be answered honestly
That's when I took possession of my insecurity

I hoped that our relationship would survive this fatal blow
For we both had a strong will and quite stubborn as you know
The process would take great strength if we were both to grow
But once we both conceded our lives began to flow

If we accept our aspirations as not being quite the same
We will allow one another to acquire our personal fame
Replacing envy and poor judgment with respect and self esteem
We'll honor individuals without greed as captain of our team

Read Between the Lines

I stopped listening to the people who try to hurt me with their lies
The *Holy Spirit* guides me to read between the lines?
I wondered what to look for and why was I so blind?
Now I see the answers that took years for me to find

The words were said to hurt me I stored them all inside!
I fed them with my fears as they formed no compromise
I thought myself a failure not worth more than a dime
I adopted all your judgments as exalted and sublime

Soon I started thinking and queried others for some clues
I found I wasn't a failure it was a just your point of view
If I would take a spot light and shine it back on you
I think we'd clearly see you have your problems too

You tried to use projection to give them all to me
Now I will assure you perhaps you will agree
If you question your past thoughts and use only honesty
You fed your pessimism so our goals could never be

Perhaps if you observe from a different paradigm
Stop pointing with your fingers and start to honor what is mine
With openness and honesty we will both have a clear view
The doubt that you may carry I'll no longer share with you

Rather than taking responsibility for our part in a failed relationship, we often carry out the old adage, "I won't get mad, I'll just get even." While this philosophy may give us a sense of satisfaction, it only manages to bring out the worst in our character, leaving us with a sense of loss and emptiness. We grow scars of resentment and distrust, which we often carry over to our next relationship. Then when we find ourselves back in the same place, we continue to blame the other party for hurting us. If we were to examine our own behavior, we might realize that we created our mess.

We often attract what we fear the most. Bradley was a good looking man with a thriving business. He took great pride in his ability to conquer every female he approached. However, his jealousy and dishonesty became his heritage. Though he was handsome and successful, he could not seem to hold on to a lasting relationship.

In the beginning, he was a great lover and friend, always acting as though he were a white knight saving a damsel in distress. Upon examination of his conquests, it became apparent that he would always target women who had little or no family support, thus making him their means of support. He wanted the frail spirited, Barbie doll type, knowing that he could put her on a shelf on any given day. He would first charm her into a false feeling of security, and then he would create chaos by playing with her vulnerability. He would transfer guilt to his victim by making her feel inadequate and incompetent, then go out on safari to bag another trophy for his game room.

He could not recognize that his lack of respect for women was actually manifested from his feeling of inferiority and loneliness. Once a partner showed any sort of assertiveness, he would immediately turn the table with accusations and innuendos. If he didn't get his way, his anger would turn to violence. When he was confronted with a firm "no," he would run away. His weakness stemmed from his fear of losing control, and ultimately he would end up in another failed relationship.

Unfortunately, it was only when Bradley suffered a heart attack that he was able to come to grips with his fear. He found that his hypertension was a result of the anxiety he brought on himself when he was not in complete control of his environment and everyone in it. What he was failing to grasp was that if he had shared his vulnerable side and not made his relationships a competition, he could have held on to the very thing he wanted most, which was a relationship filled with love and understanding. Instead, he allowed his unfounded distrust and jealous accusations to consume him. His guilt became his nemesis.

"Happiness depends on ourselves." –*Aristotle*

Eye for and Eye

An eye for an eye is merely a *perception!*
One that's been misread
We've taught our cultures these deceptions
Which soon could cause our death
We changed the sacred words
And define them to meet our means
But if the *truth* be known …
They are worth no more than beans!
To pluck the eye from one mans head
For the vengeance of a brother
Will only leave a generation
Of one blind man with another
If we open our hearts and souls
To make *God's* meaning clear
Our martyrs would be alive
And we'd be full of Cheer!
I hope we'll recognize before it is too late!
That it's only through our giving *love*
That we will *free* ourselves of hate!
Salvation comes when we look
Through Spirits eyes as *God* does see us all as one
Living under gracious skies
For it is that clear vision that peeps through a pure eye
The fog of these deceptions I hope will claim its toll
So clarity and sanity can tunnel like a mole!
The blinders may be lifted
And sunlight will shine through
To expose the loving happiness
That is meant for me and you
It is to this vibration that we must *resonate*
For if we don't practice … what we *preach!*
It may become too *LATE!*

Familiarity often breeds contempt. Ann and Roger made no bones about how they felt for each other. They had been married for 25 years, and over a period of time they became very relaxed in their tone of voice. They would interrupt one another to correct the other's perception of a story. Soon it was so out of control that their friends began to comment, questioning the state of their marriage.

One day, Ann had enough of Roger's back talk and rude interruptions. She land blasted him in the middle of a story while they were having lunch with friends. But the looks of sheer surprise on their faces stopped her cold. She was embarrassed and ashamed of her actions. What caused this couple, who had shared a quarter of a century together, to become so indifferent to each other's feelings?

Over the years, they gradually became comfortable with the daily routine; they took for granted that things would always remain the same. Unfortunately, life has an uncanny way of stepping in to stir up the mix when change is needed. Ann and Roger were products of the 60s, when the mind set for married couples was still somewhat stuck in the old belief that a woman was to stay at home, tending to the family. Ann could've joined her emancipated peers, burning her bra and entering the corporate world to pursue a career. She was clearly caught in a dilemma. She stayed at home with her family in the early years. But when the children were finally out of the house, she felt a definite void, an emptiness for her purpose.

Roger failed to see her plight and was completely insensitive to Ann's needs. After all, he was enjoying his life. He received undivided attention, his meals were on time, the house was clean, the laundry was washed and folded, and his physical needs were always satisfied. What could Ann have to complain about? When Ann approached Roger about starting an outside job, he took a stance of passive resistance, using criticism and sarcasm to undermine Ann's self esteem. Ann felt she was not capable of doing anything meaningful, other than taking care of Roger.

Thinking it would kill two birds with one stone, Roger allowed Ann to start a mail order business from their home.

Ann was supposed to consult Roger about every decision, because his fear of losing control was not going to allow her to think for herself. When she objected, he began to pout and demanded more and more of her time, wanting her to sit with him while watching TV or working on his hobby. He didn't want her to talk, just to sit. Ann began to resent his selfishness and started to do her own thing, in spite of Roger's moods. This made Roger even more difficult to be with. He would criticize nearly everything she attempted. Her self esteem was slowly being broken down to where she could hardly make a decision without running it by Roger first. As a result, she became extremely resentful and frustrated with the entire situation.

They unwittingly took their frustrations out on each other in the simplest of fashions, which soon escalated from verbal barbs and snipes to public confrontations. Roger and Ann became increasingly bitter and seemed to lose all respect for one another. They lost their desire to communicate, not realizing that their fear of losing their relationship was becoming a slowly growing reality. It is not easy to release one's control over another, and it does take time, but if it is not accomplished the end result is not very pretty. Couples who once thought nothing in the world could separate them end up divorced or living a miserable co-existence due to their persistent efforts to be right rather than happy.

"The worst loneliness is not to be comfortable with yourself."– Mark Twain

Things you said

The awful things you said to me I most likely won't forget!
I am told I must release them or for sure I will regret
If I lock the hate inside me it will cause me great despair
For a time I did resent you this I will declare

While I took your words inside me and held them to my heart
I've learned a precious lesson … and I'm glad that we're apart
I forgive you for this drama for there's one thing I realize
You will pay a painful Karma for all your nasty lies

I know it won't be easy especially for me …
My ego wants to hate you but it's not serving me!
You bruised my self esteem the day you walked away
I did not see it coming so nothing went my way!

I thought that we were happy and, failed to see that you
Were going through the motions for friends and family too
Perhaps there is no fault here we both just did not see
That we were slowly drifting from our responsibility

There is a painful truth here everyone should know
Once we shift our paradigms our lives will surely grow
In time we might communicate if we don't transfer the blame
And use words of true forgiveness void of all the shame

So let's not burn our bridges because we're both in pain
We mustn't feed these demons that make us act insane
Instead we must release them so a peace there might/could be
And this will likely happen when we *agree to disagree!*

Relationships should not be strained, with one party trying to please the other due to a fear of abandonment or loss of control. Relationships need to be a work in progress, not a work to process.

When Michelle and John met, they were both rebounding from long term relationships, and eager to regain a sense of belonging and companionship. Unfortunately, both were still so wounded emotionally that neither recognized the danger in entering a new relationship. They were not only deceiving each other about their denial, they were also deceiving themselves.

John was a good looking, successful young man with a winning personality. He was able to date just about any woman he chose. Michelle was a beautiful young woman with a kind, vulnerable heart. She had been taken advantage of by her last boyfriend, both financially and emotionally, and unbeknownst to her she was about to fall into the same trap. John persistently preyed on her vulnerability, until she finally gave in. It was not long before they moved in together. Then the games began.

Michelle looked at John as the little boy she was destined to save from himself, and he looked at her as the mother he had always wanted, but with a few fringe benefits. Both served each other's purpose, until they soon needed some space. Then the monsters of jealousy and possession reared their ugly heads. Neither John nor Michelle was able to enjoy an evening with friends without having the other along. Soon, the feelings of entrapment and resentment began to suffocate them. Their communication broke down, and nasty innuendos and accusations became part of their normal conversation.

They both had skeletons from their pasts that they were either unaware of, or just did not recognize. The fighting got worse, and soon the relationship ended in a separation, which neither really wanted. When they came to see me, John had been ordered by the court because of his inability to control his anger. Michelle was a button pusher and needed to learn how to get her message across without nagging. John was suffering from an over inflated ego and was desperately trying to conceal his emotions. He would dominate all conversations, defending his actions and transferring his guilt to whoever was within earshot.

Michelle was so emotionally battered that she repressed her anger, allowing it to smolder like coals on a BBQ, and then she would withdraw into a quiet shell, leaving John with the feeling of a conquering warrior. Fortunately, when they separated, Michelle sought counseling and in eight months she was able to regain her personal power. Although she was still dating John, they no longer lived together. John, on the other hand, jumped from one woman to another. He finally realized that he could date any woman he wanted, but he could not keep even one. His lies and deceptions would always catch up with him. John was drowning in a river of denial, and he was lonely and confused.

Michelle knew that John would not change over night, but she saw his better side and decided to seek counseling with him to either work out their relationship as a couple or remain friends. Either way, she knew that if she wanted to have peace, she needed to have closure on her demons or she would be doomed to repeat the same mistakes.

"Mistakes obviously show us what needs improving. Without mistakes how would we know what we had to work on?" –
Peter Mc Williams, "Life 101"

Carney Ride

Life is like a *Carney Ride* it has its ups and downs
We play with our emotions like pups and circus clowns
But why do we pass judgment?
With, scorn and awkward frowns
Life is like a *Carney Ride* it has its ups and downs

I try to understand it and spare all judgment from the past
If there's to be a future …
A new vision we must cast
The past it holds us hostage from a future we might know
Happiness is our Destiny not things from long ago

We store these thoughts in boxes where fear begins to grow
Our hearts begin to shutter at thoughts that might be ours
The rules were carefully patterned
Like fine *Cuban Cigars!*
Life is like a *Carney Ride* it has its ups and downs

It's time to jump this crazy ride
Shedding ego and false pride
If we recognize these patterns
We will deal with what's inside
Life is like a *Carney Ride* it has its ups and downs

Soul Mate

When you think you've meet your soul mate
You might just look again to see
For the one you thought was flawless
May not really be …

Your lessons would be easy
If your paths were paved with gold
You'd see through the illusion
Rather than waiting until you're old

When discussing with your soul mate
The things you think should be
Don't be surprised if their decision
Is construed quite differently

You will both voice an opinion
For there is no right or wrong
So when in closing a discussion
Be kind but always strong

Or you'll make the same mistakes
And it won't be very long
Until you'll both be singing
A sad old country song!

Soul Journey

I sat around and wrote one day
My thoughts were all of you
Your love and giving ways
Were often in my view
I sometimes wondered why?
You took my subtle blows
To experience these lessons
Must have caused you many woes!

But now I understand
That with each little bit of pain
You were storing a new energy
So your kingdom you could reign
Now that you are wiser and your power is in force
I see I was the weak one that owes you some remorse
I boasted with my ego and overconfidence
I lost my friends and partners I had no common sense

My life was so transparent to everyone but me
I fed my selfish ego like a dog would feed a flea
It's time to buy a ticket and give direction to my soul
I'll admit to indiscretions or I'll never get control
I'll change these wrong perceptions
For they'll surely take their toll
I pray these revelations
Will give us peace and make us whole!

Sticks and stones may break my bones, but words will never hurt me! How often have we heard this catchy little tune? Unfortunately, the sticks and stones may have broken bones, and left some scars. The misguided words of an angry, controlling, or jealous person often leave wounds embedded in our soul, only to surface years later, manifesting themselves in repressed anger, road rage, addictions, and many other dysfunctional behaviors. I remember having a disagreement with a colleague. I was determined to hold firm to my opinion. My intuitive mind was telling me that it was not what my colleague was saying; it was how she was saying it. I don't remember the reason for the disagreement, but I do remember the incident.

That night I meditated on the incident, and I recalled a similar situation where my father used the same tone with me. I was a teenager at the time, and I was tired of my father's unreasonable harassment, so I made a promise to myself that I would never allow anyone to disrespect me by talking down to me again. As a consequence, I was not listening to my colleague's words, only her tone. It did not matter how right she may have been, because her words were falling on deaf ears. Verbal abuse will often do more harm than physical abuse, because we tend to unconsciously store the painful words in our subconscious minds, only to have the consequences surface years later. Criticism is often internalized, rather than recognized as being constructive and perceived as a vicious attack. What we fail to see is that the people who love us the *best* will tell us what we need to hear, not what we want to hear. Even when words are said in anger, if we were to reflect on their value rather than the pain, valuable lessons would be revealed. We are so busy feeding our defensive ducks that we fail to listen to the true message.

Accepting criticism is possibly one of the hardest things a person can deal with, especially when they are putting forth what they feel is a great effort. The trick is not to take criticism as a personal affront. Change the thought to one of gratitude by looking at the person as a teacher. This person sees greatness in you that you may have overlooked. One man's criticism, if perceived differently, could be another man's praise.

Jarvis was a black belt in karate, competing in a national tournament. His coach was standing on the sidelines, barking out his commands when a young spectator called out to him in a rather firm voice. She asked if he had ever considered changing his tone of voice and body language. The spectator's criticism took the coach back a few steps, because he never really thought about his behavior. Later that evening over dinner, the coach asked Jarvis if he felt that he was being harsh in his criticism.

Jarvis told him, "No, not anymore, but at first I felt there was nothing I could do right. Later, I realized that you just wanted the best for me. So now I ignore your tone, and only listen to your direction. Although, I suppose if a stranger were listening, it could be perceived as rude. After all, I'm on the mat getting my ass kicked, and you're on the sidelines asking me why I'm allowing it to happen."

I guess people don't always see things in the same light.

"If indeed you must be candid, be candid beautifully."
—Kahlil Gibran

Telescope

I had a Telescope and often used to play
I watched the Stars from Planets and Comets fly away
I looked into the emptiness for diamonds on black skies
And realized this same emptiness was revealed in your brown eyes
Perhaps you didn't notice how deeply I would Probe
Like looking through your eardrum and seeing lobe to lobe
I noticed your affection although you may not have seen
You have a talent for perfection that some perceived as mean!
To appreciate another without looking at the Past!
Puts you far above all others and that's how friendships last
You go beyond the judgment and accept me *Just for Me!*

For this I will always thank you for allowing me to *Be!*
You give me so much confidence I don't think you realize
How much it really means to me to see that twinkle in your eyes
For those who are not savvy to how you show your Love
I fear that they are missing the insight from above
Through you I learned that judgment
Is something to restrain for often the true picture
Will come without a frame so now I use my telescope
And look between the Stars
And that is where you'll see what's hiding
Between Venus and Oh, yes *Mars!*

Charlene came to me for hypnosis to help her let go of her fear of speaking to an audience. One on one, or sitting in a small group, she was a dynamite speaker, but when it came to speaking to more than 5 or 6 people she would freeze up. During one of her sessions she recalled an incident from her grammar school music class. She was embarrassed by her teacher for singing solo after the entire class had stopped. She was so involved in the song that she had closed her eyes and proceeded to belt out her tune. She soon realized that she was the only one singing. She opened her eyes to see a giggling audience of 7 year olds who offered derogatory comments about her performance. She wanted to crawl under the table, and to further her embarrassment her teacher added her two cents of ridicule.

At that very moment, Charlene decided that she would never allow herself to be embarrassed like that again. From then on, whenever she was asked to stand and read aloud to her classmates, she would freeze. She would stammer, and her mouth would feel like a bowl of cotton balls. After our session, she realized that she was allowing a 7 year old to limit her ability to come forward and be heard. People frequently turn their dreams to nightmares when, through no fault of their own, or I should say no memory of their own, they end up storing unpleasant events from their past and allowing them to create their futures.

By holding on to our past beliefs and judgments, we limit ourselves to the mentality of a flat world. In the broader scheme of things, we allow our minds to be governed by the thoughts and beliefs of others by taking their ideas and theories as facts, which few dare to challenge. As a result, we get stuck in the old world cultures and myths, finding ourselves dwelling on fears of the unknown.

Thank God for the few who crossed the finish line and went on to explore new territories and navigate new seas. If it weren't for these adventurers, we very well might be fashioning our automobile tires from marble. Learn from the past, but don't allow it to control your future. It is not necessary to follow *every* leader. One would do well to keep an open mind, accepting the differences of our fellow men, and if not willing to adopt another point of view, then tolerate it if it is not causing undue harm to others. If this was not God's intention, then I must wonder why He created so many diverse races, languages, and nationalities. It would seem that we were meant to transcend our myths and inherited traditions to evolve into a race absent of hostilities and anxieties, experiencing the joy of discovering new territories and horizons that we once felt were unattainable.

"To live is so startling it leaves little time for anything else."
Emily Dickinson

The Secret

There is an Ancient Secret that lies within the Soul
It's hidden and suppressed like the bridge that hides the Troll!
It is seeded with a thought and starts to come in view
Then Manifests to action when fed by energy too
Your life would be much better and peace will come to you
Once you change your way of thinking
And adopt another point of view!
Start facing everyday with thoughts of Gratitude
And you'll attract a positive change with this new Attitude
Now some may not believe me for in the past they want to stay
Preaching and defending their perceptions of "*The Way*"
So just cling to what is useful and throw away the rest
Our Guides and Masters they will teach us …
To acknowledge what is best …
When we consult our inner souls we'll recognize their lessons
For its inside we hide the clues …
That will allow us no concessions
By invoking Source's aid we will never lose
It is in that sleepy cavern … that we will learn to choose
We'll come to know the answers to all our private questions
And for certain we will grow …
Bringing happiness to our sessions
By things we thought we knew …
And affirmations for our missions

Manifested Fears

Don't feed your fears they'll ruin you
And you'll repeat your past
For yesterday you can't redo or the fog will surely last
This Karma you have chosen you must clear it up for sure!
Or you will just repeat it with a healthy dose of more!
Your sins may seem so many but do they belong to you?
For there's some you did inherit from Dad or Mom that's true
They say that education will tend to clear your view
Or do you just inherit another point of view?

God gave you a *free will* you chose your selfishness
Somewhere along the way you lost your *self- less-ness*
You bought into a *Dogma* that allowed no thoughts from you
It enslaved you in a *Doctrine* with a narrow point of view
Well now I'm here to tell you of a choice that you can take
To free yourself of bondage will release you
From a terminal mistake!
If it's love that you were seeking stop boarding up the door
With your fear and your deception about what you're looking for

By making a commitment you thought I'd take your wealth
That was the wrong conclusion you can put that one on a shelf
Since we're not together I hope that you have learned
My devotion and pure love for you was my ultimate concern
I had hopes to raise our family…
Without doubts and fearful cries I see now this won't happen
Because our life was built on lies!
The things you've manifested you managed to attract
The likelihood of change will be revealed by your next act!

Free Will

Some say we're all your children and that we must obey
And like all good parents you'll guide us all the way
At times we'll disobey you and for sure we're gonna pay
But when all is said and done you'll love us anyway
When I put my eyes upon you, there's only one thing I can say
If life is but a whisper you took my breath away

I bonded with you *Spirit* from deep within my soul
Now I have this illness I will surely let you know
It's not what I was thinking of to help myself to grow
But here in lies a lesson from a weakness I did sow
Forgiveness is my healing as you pointed out to me
I will do a lot of sharing too teach responsibility

With unconditional love it seems obvious to me
That I would take this burden and carry it so free
I'm sure that this affliction as dire as it seems
Will only make me stronger as I see what real love means
My inner flame is growing a new courage from within
I'll turn away your pity as you smile an impish grin

I pray that you'll stay with me and instruct me as I teach
To Forgive and Understand especially to those who preach
Their minds were put in boxes being told they couldn't think
But freewill is our present a gift that's quite distinct
We've been given this gift of love
Without punishment or shame our freewill gives us choices
It's our Ego we must tame!

Life's Illusions

When you watch a movie
It's all a … private show
Sometimes you'll know the ending
Or you'll never know!

Life is like a movie
And it is your private show!
Write the script you want for you
And watch the actors go

Watch your words *Be Careful!*
For they will tell the truth
The truth that hides inside you
Reveals the scholar or the *Goof!*

Thoughts are things we cling to
The things we fear to Share.
And as we watch this movie
The *Illusion* will appear

Now, you must not worry!
For you can change this script
Because you are the writer
The Master so well … *Equipped!*

W
N
S
E

Shift

I've heard your petty gossip and all of your problems too!
You'd like me at your level but that I just won't do
You've spread my name in shame …
And have shown me no remorse
I will play your game no longer I have chosen a new course!
For karma you will pay it and a handsome sum it's true
You've wrapped yourself in lies … Oh, they'll catch up with you!
It's not punishment I'm speaking it is the consequence
You'll find that the deceitful lies are climbing up your fence

Now you may make excuses of which, I'm sure you're good
To form a real alliance perhaps a brotherhood
With those who will support you for they may play your game
They may seek a pact with you of which you'll sink in shame
I have turned my heart to *Spirit* and opened my mind too
I see right through the Dogma and the judgment it can do!
If we're to be a family and share this world in Peace
The fear, shame, blame and hatred …
We will *"All"* have to release!

All books of Scripture tell us that we must love the same
So why is it we're fighting?
Then claim it's in *God's* name!
Why can't we pay attention to what is happening here
Our lands are in destruction all because of *Fear*
If we would share our riches as we do this awful Pain
There would be no devastation no famine and no lame
We chose all this destruction our change it must be *Swift!*
For our Souls to see Salvation we will have to make a *Shift!*

Have you ever experienced a dream that was so real that it made you wonder if you were actually living the experience? We waste so much time worrying about the things we have no control over that we fail to appreciate the present moment.

We allow our prejudice and narrow minded opinions to cloud our judgment, and before we know it our life is over. Our legacies accomplish small reversals of inherited dilemmas which seldom reach the core issues as we swim in our sea of denial. We gorge ourselves on ego satisfying habits and traditions, and then we wonder where peace has gone.

Robin Williams starred in the movie "What Dreams will Come" about ten years ago. In it he went to hell in an effort to save his already deceased wife from eternal damnation. She had given up all hope of salvation, for the thought of never seeing her family again was much too overwhelming to accept. I won't go through the entire movie, but the point being made was to never give up, and that life is a continuum and the illusion death. Our souls may leave this earthly realm, but we have the ability to travel to new worlds, learn new things, and experience all our dreams. Whether or not you believe in the afterlife doesn't really matter, the bottom line is that if you allow doubt to enter your consciousness, all your possibilities will be limited.

To paraphrase the Bible – "If you have faith the size of a mustard seed, you shall move mountains."

It's no secret that the rich get richer and the poor get welfare. The law of attraction is very clear on how it operates. It is important to understand that thoughts are things and we manifest the things we think about by planting seeds with each thought. As children, we're apt to adopt the thought patterns of our families, then our churches, and then our cultures. Only when we are exposed to new ideas and philosophies are the gateways to change opened. Whether we choose to change or stay in the familiar groove of mediocrity is entirely up to the individual. One would think that most people would want to make a permanent life change for the better. However, some people are afraid to take a step out of their comfort zone, not necessarily for fear of failure, but more for fear of success. If they make it then they have to keep it; this holds true in both personal and business relationships.

This myth, if not dispelled, will cause many talented people to give up on their dreams and become consumed by failure. The phrase "With my luck things will go wrong" is all too familiar, and when projected to the Universe it is taken as a request and therefore granted. Many relationships fail because of this mind set. Most second marriages fall prey to the same malfunction as the first, because they fail to change their preconceived notion that if it's not working then they must move on. This proves the old adage that if you keep doing what you have always done, you will keep getting what you have always gotten.

The solution is quite simple; however, it's not quite so easy. If you are not 100 percent committed to changing your past behaviors, then the past results will not change either.

You'll wander from relationship to relationship or job to job with all the best intentions, only to find yourself right back at the starting gate, confronting new faces with the same old ideas. This holds true with addictions, because at first you have a sense of security and comfort. Gradually, as your fear of losing control becomes even more apparent, you begin to perceive others as a threat. So you move on to what you imagine, new frontiers, relationships, or addictions, always finding a sense of security in the haven you've built with your lies. You surround yourself with safe people who will feed your addictions and your self serving ego, telling you what you want, rather than what you need.

When help is offered, you reject it by rationalizing your behavior and transferring the blame to someone else. Soon you find yourself in a most uncomfortable place of despair, dissolution, and depression, dressed in masks of arrogance, denial, and a false sense of security, which you further feed by preying on those who are weaker than you or compassionate to your cause. Soon, they see through your games, and you ultimately find yourself surrounded by new faces with the same problems.

Clifford got his first DUI when he was 21. Unfortunately, it was not his first encounter with alcohol. He had been drinking for several years prior to this incident, and he was a nasty drunk. When I met him he had already been in three fights that put him in the hospital, causing him extensive debt and pain. He attended a few anger management classes, but never took them seriously. He was not ready or willing to admit to his addiction, and paranoid that everyone in his life was out to get him.

When clients are referred to me by the court, it's usually either because of a DUI or domestic abuse with anger issues. The first thing I ask is whether they want to change, or are they just coming to the class because they were ordered by a judge. If they say it is because they were ordered by the judge, I know I am more than likely dealing with someone who is in a great deal of denial. If they have been ordered to take only a few hours, I will refer them to someone else. I will only deal with clients who are serious about making a positive change in their lives, and even then a few will slip through the cracks. However, all of them came from homes with either substance or physical abuse. I'm sad to say that not all of them were able beat their addictions. Jenny's father was an alcoholic who gambled, chased women, and he also had an anger problem. Her mother was a subservient woman, grasping at any opportunity she could to prove her independence. She was her husband's partner in business, as well as the mother of his three children. Their household was in constant turmoil, and their three girls were always getting mixed messages on how a family should be.

On one hand, they were attending private schools, attending church every Sunday, and going to after school programs. They even sold cookies at fund raisers. From the outside, Jenny's family looked like a Norman Rockwell painting. But, neither Jenny nor any of her sisters would bring a friend home after school for fear of what they might walk in on. The masquerade was successful, right up to Jenny's youngest sister's high school graduation. Once the last girl was out of the house, Jenny's mother filed for divorce and then she left the state. She knew that her daughters were fine on their own, and she wanted nothing to do with her husband again. The game was over.

Jenny stayed in her home town, married to her high school sweetheart. She had two children and led the Norman Rockwell life. Her middle sister Morgan left home, and then she went on to college, where she graduated with reasonably good grades. She married the boss and joined him as a partner in their marketing firm. Her youngest sister Bernice moved to the West coast and had little contact with her family for several years. Oddly enough, all three girls married or had relationships with men exactly like their father. Each girl saw her dad in a different light, and molded their mates to their perceived roles.

If a weakness or flaw would surface, Jenny would immediately address it by consulting a counselor or clergymen, always making sure her husband was proactive in keeping their line of communication open. Morgan handled her conflicts by working harder, putting in more hours and becoming super woman, but never really addressing her issues. She was always afraid of developing an addiction to alcohol or gambling, so she made sure that her time and money were always working for her. Bernice drifted from one man to another, never establishing any solid relationships, always one step away from disaster.

Despite our unpleasant experiences, we have all been gifted with free will. It is our individual choice as to how we will create our future. Everyone has a story. Perhaps you will relate to yours, recognize its value, and then change what may have been a thought of imminent doom to one of success and encouragement. The important thing to remember is that the ultimate choice is yours. I will continue to reiterate throughout this book that your thoughts are things, and through those thoughts you will manifest the things you want. The challenge is to know what you want and be clear about it.

Fear is one of the most common causes of anger. We are creatures of habit and find a sense of comfort in what we know. So as a result, we return to our addictions, stay in unhealthy relationships, join gangs, stay in a job we don't like, stay with the family business that we have no real interest in, and continue to embrace the familiar parts of our world. Rather than stepping out in faith, we cling to warm fuzzy slippers or emotional teddy bears. When we fall short of a goal, we automatically say, "Well, that's it. I tried and it didn't work, so I will go back to what I know." Then we blame someone or something else for our failure.

Looking back at my friends and acquaintances, I've found that the people who came from the most advantaged homes were the people who seldom satisfied their true passion. The sons of doctors, lawyers, teachers and preachers often followed in their parent's career desires. What was even more interesting was that all the money and time their parents spent on providing a well rounded education (music, dance, and art lessons), it usually resulted in well intended hobbies that eventually ended up stored away in an attic, basement, or scrap book with memories of what could have been. Yet, people with parents who seemed not as obsessed with the outcome of their children usually pursued their dreams and went on to find happiness in what they wanted, not what was wanted for them.

If you are going to allow someone else to throw cold water on your dreams, they will drown. It is the well intending husband, wife, friend, or sibling who is most likely to remind you of the things you can't or shouldn't do. Why would they do this? After all, these are the people closest to you. One would think that of all the support systems out there, your family and friends would be at the top of your list. This is not necessarily true. Your family and friends are either afraid to see you fail, or they are afraid you might succeed. Either way, they might lose a possession or lose control. If you fail, they won't want to see you suffer the pain of defeat. If you succeed, you may no longer need them or want them in your world. What people fail to realize is that if you're not encouraged to pursue your dreams, then everyone has lost.

If you give up, then you will always wonder what might have been. What would life be like if you had done this or that? In many cases, you harbor a deep resentment for people who held you back from your dreams. This resentment manifests itself in relationships, jobs, and in new opportunities to advance or change lifestyles.

"The aim of life is self-development. To realize one's nature perfectly, that is what we are here for" – *Oscar Wilde*

Revelation

I slipped into a Coma at first it was a fright!
Then I found some comfort like sleeping through the night
I watched all those around me scrambling in the lane!
As they scraped me off the pavement!
Thinking, I must be in great pain …
It was like a play I was watching or a movie too
For there were many characters some of which I knew
My whole life went before me and that was quite a show!
Oh! There were Revelations I didn't want to know!
I saw from where I'd come and what I could have been
If I had just applied myself I may have been Gunga Din!

My life I made Chaotic I created it with lies
Only to find out that it would lead to my demise
I lived in Fame and Glory which I did not create
I used deceit and hatred to build *My Pearly Gate!*
My spirit sits beside my shell and looks into my eyes!
I see what I don't want to be and clearly do despise!
If Grace be granted to me and I am allowed to live
I make this promise to you from now on *"I will Give!"*
My life is one so peaceful and violence they'll be none
I will turn the other cheek when presented with a gun
My sins of past were many and of the present too
But it's a viewing of my Future that I am showing you

My work will be to correlate this different point of view
To bring the peace of Jesus Christ, Gandhi and Martin too
We ask you for forgiveness Father, we know not what we do
For if we are all equal as we are supposed to be
We must recognize and believe in our own true deity
The one that works for you may not be the one for *ME!*
It doesn't really matter what his name is going to be
Weather it be Christ, Krishna, Buddha, Mohammad or Alai?
Our paths will come together when we worship just one GOD

Tool Box

Create a craftsman's toolbox
With friends that won't relate
Or sympathize with your complaints
And help you to … *sedate*

Choose people who will tell you
Things you *don't* want to hear
Who will share with you the truth
So you can face your fear

You will know that they do love you
For they accept you as you are
And have the strength and courage
To take your keys and then your car

Destiny

If we choose our Parents our Siblings and our Friends
We do this to learn lessons or just to make amends
Our lives make many changes the road may show a curve
We never know the out come and often loose our nerve

Our suits they have no pockets we dress along the way
We choose the things we want and all the games we'll play!
Sometimes we may help others only to get hurt
Which ever way the coin is tossed we will get our just desert

I may not be the first one but this I'll guarantee
If I hurt someone today it will surely come back to me!
While that might be the bad news there is some good news too
When I give respect and kindness it makes that circle to

My choice is to forgive them for the sins they put on me
Although, they seemed horrific our healing is the key
Now look to *God's* perfection forgiveness says it all
And have no time for *Anger* its not something to applaud

Remember what we're here for you see we are all the same!
Angels were delivered and wore the humans name
We had no hats or coats not even a pair of boots
Exposures were all different but we all had the same roots

From God we were delivered we were angels all the same
We came to learn our lessons and no one was to blame
We were made all of perfection a seed from the divine
A thorn-less rose of beauty its flawless from *God's* loin!

Trust your path

Trust the path you've chosen
For you picked it long ago
You looked for Mom and Dad
As a tiny embryo

You're like brush strokes on a canvas
A magnificent work of art
You chose all those around you
Yes…each and every part

So, now don't start complaining
For it's a senseless mood
You must complete
What you are planning

Just change your attitude!

I meditate every morning, which I find especially helpful when I have something troubling me or an important decision to make. My mind travels to a special place that I visited when I was a child. We lived in the mountains, and behind our house was a small creek. When my parents argued, I would retreat to this special place to find solace. The sweet music of the water, gently making its way over the rocks, and the stream of sunlight filtering through the trees always sent a peaceful feeling to my soul. It was so nice to hear the tree frogs and "Katie did its" playing their instrument of love, honoring the unconditional acceptance of what is.

I would watch the butterflies share the sweet nectar of wild flowers, as spiders methodically weaved their silky grids in preparation for the evening meal. I never felt threatened, even when an occasional snake would slither past me, sometimes mistaking my foot for a rock. It would stop and then look up, as though it knew I was just a visitor who was enjoying its well furnished living room. Then it would continue on its path, looking for a warm rock to heat its quilt patterned body. I was at peace to sift through and process my thoughts. It seemed that no matter how upset I was, or how chaotic my home life could be, I knew that God was beside me, always guiding me through the rough spots in the form of my intuitive inner thoughts.

As a teenager and young adult, I tried using alcohol to numb the pain and stress of my home life. I would somehow always come to my senses, knowing deep inside that there was a reason for this experience, and if I would stay strong, God would reveal a lesson. It became clear that the lesson was unconditional forgiveness and love for all those whom I thought had offended me. In lieu of sounding righteous, I admit that my lessons were many, and not always learned the first time around.

As Buddhists believe, *"When the student is ready the teacher will appear."* Once I was willing to use *my* mind to explore, and I refrained from holding any judgment toward different cultures, religions, and traditions, my world opened up to liberate my fears of inadequacy and insecurity, and I was freed. I became like a sponge, thirsty for news and seeking new ideas and objectives to fulfill my goals and happiness. I am open to listening with both ears, rather than formulating answers to questions that were not mine.

"I have learnt silence from the talkative, toleration from the intolerant, and kindness from the unkind; yet I am ungrateful to these teachers." -Kahlil Gibran

Fountain of Truth

The water from this fountain is meant for soothing you
The night lights and the mists are for the babies too
In water there is a power one may not often see
It carves its way through Canyons and travels to the Sea

God gives you strength from water it's a gift to nourish you
It cleans you from the inside and your outer body too
Don't ever take for granted what His substance can do for you
It comes in many forms as you already knew

It cools you in the summer it gives you play time too
It's just a small reminder of the wonders you can view
As it slips right through your fingers you may miss a thing or two
The tears you shed alone will bring a cleansing all to you

It may be time for Re-birth a fresh new start for you
Just as water is a constant we are always here for you
Our love it runs so deep like springs beneath the ground
Know we are always with you even if we're not around!

Our Spirits are connected like blue skies with white clouds
We are glad to be your parents for you make us oh so… Proud!
We watch you in the bad times getting back up on your feet
With kindness and compassion there is nothing you can't defeat

Forgiveness is like water that *Spirit* gives to you
The insight to dissolve and release the hurt you're holding to
There'll be no more conditions and your dreams will all come true
By releasing your resentment you'll regain your freedom too

So see this as a lesson from a classroom way above
You're building a whole new strength through *unconditional* Love!
Now when you view this *Fountain* I hope that you will see
The subtle little reminder of all that you can be!

For generations we have been fighting wars for various reasons, like boundary disputes, both civil and international sects of religious factions, races, ethnic backgrounds, and defending our pride and prejudices for one reason or another. If we were to take an impartial look at our true motives and agendas, it might be discovered that we are a race of greedy people. There is never enough. Each nation, culture, religious sect, and ethnic group is suffering from a severe case of "Bigger, better, more" dis-ease!

I will admit that it is nice to have possessions, yet what may seem comfortable to one may not satisfy another. I'm not saying to settle for little or nothing; I'm saying that it's time to get things in perspective and figure out what we as a human race need, not what we want. For our wants will always *out-want* our needs, unless we learn to *honor* everyone's right to coexist. Rather than feel that it is our duty to make their world acceptable to our definition, there will always be a superior being with the perception of what is needed as a cure all for mankind.

Confusion is caused when we attach ourselves to a belief and are not willing to accept reality as what is *real*. While we may fight for our *right to be right,* we may also keep in mind that battles are seen as lessons that wars may end. By choosing to understand that our thoughts are no more or less valid than those of another, we will learn to accept our foes as friends. Their actions, whether good or bad, can then be seen as *gifts* sent by God, Source, or Holy Spirit, whoever our higher power might be. These gifts are meant to reveal the truth about unconditional love, making it as simple as the reality of what has happened, thus opening new portals for change. The following "story poems" are intended to reflect these feelings and open the possibility to new thoughts and paradigms. Reality is what has happened, and for the most part we cannot change what has already happened. However, by recognizing our role in recreating our past behaviors, we can stop them from becoming a repetitive future.

Nations and empires, families and friends have succumbed to fateful disasters for fear of losing control of what was familiar, and reaped their most dreaded punishments. From the beginning of time we have distorted the meaning of God's love. Just as a mother would unconditionally love her child, the Universe, or God, whatever name one may choose, would love us.

Yet, we are consumed by the urge to force our individual belief systems on those around us. We wage wars, divide governments, and split families just to enforce what we perceive as the only path to heaven. We cheat on our spouses, governments steal from their constituents, preachers and teachers molest our children, and if there is enough political clout or financial backing, all is pardoned. If one should have a different religious value or belief than that of the local population, they most likely will be shunned or inundated by well meaning prophets who persist that they accept and testify to their particular dogma.

God is a constant life force where there is no judgment, only a source of unconditional love and forgiveness for all. He or she will become nameless, once recognized as the Source for all mankind. If we continue to stay stuck in our past stories, we may miss the reasons and valuable learning experiences that were originally intended. If this were to happen we could very well be doomed to a life or repetitive historic wars that claim generations of innocent lives.

In his book The Path to Tranquility, the Dalai Lama offers this thought:

"Our judgments, even concerning ordinary things, are frequently clouded by our emotions. For example, we often see the actions of our loved ones—even if they are harmful—as wonderful, whereas we judge even the positive actions of a person we dislike as pretentious and false. We cannot rely upon our perceptions; it is a fact that we miscomprehend many situations. If this is a general fact, how can we still stubbornly maintain that our perceptions about our own spiritual masters must be true?"

God of Consequence

My God is one of consequence not punishment you see
For even when I'm messing up He's looking over me
I feared his wrath for many years but failed to understand
That what I really needed was to take him by the hand

For while he is my Savior … He is my mentor too
I know that he will love me no matter what I do
I respect him with great honor and receive him like a dove
For he sent me his son Jesus with his unconditional love

When Christ the Lords beside me I know that I can be
A soldier in his army allowing all souls to see
It's not my place to judge them for righteous that would be
And that is not a position that I have earned for me

I will look into my own heart and pay only for my past
I'll offer you forgiveness and honor the roll that I've been cast
Condemning and condoning oh no that's not for me
I will leave this up to Jesus Christ only he can set us free

I will practice what he taught us to love and understand
And to turn the other cheek when you smite me with your hand
I know this won't be easy for my ego must take flight
But I will recognize this devil and put Jesus in my sight

I know he walks beside me no matter what I do
But it's the times that I ignore him my troubles flood right through
So here I stand before him confessing all my sins
I'm seeking his forgiveness …

And watch him as he grins he tells me that I perfect
As he has cleansed me of my sins …
The guilt that I have taken is clearly not all mine
This world will only change when I see a new paradigm

Boy of 21

I was a Naive Soldier a boy of twenty one
I fought for Pride and Glory of which I will have none
My cause while it seemed noble I found I was misled
As my allies sprayed Agent Orange far above my Head!
They said it would not harm me of this I was assured
That it was only foliage that was being *"Scourged"!*
But, as the years have passed me I found this was Not True!
It killed my fellow Soldiers the ones like me and you

I found my skin was blistering without the flames I knew!
That something deep inside me was making its way through
My heart began to flutter my liver failed me too
This was my Biggest Battle it was a past I couldn't share with you
And now as I lie here on my death bed I've been told!
I see that at age fifty I've become so old!
My insides are one hundred give a year or two
I pray the same Mistake is not happening to you

So if you pay a dollar I have advice for you
Be careful who you follow or allow too guide you through
This world has many evils some say that they are good!
But, who is this man in Power? Who leads our brotherhood
He led us to the Desert and now it's a New Game!
We're back to Pride and Glory but this time it's in God's name!
Who really wants this power?
When it's something God does have!
So question why we're fighting … as if on His behalf?

Perhaps we are in trouble … and should take a closer view!
What is this Pride and Glory … that we are marching too?
Our Children are alone … their parents can not guide!
Our governments are feeding us … more fear to hide inside!
We need to change this theory … to one of love at least!
For that's the God I Know! And, once we do release!
By extending our forgiveness …
We will accomplish a hard earned Peace

Cultures

I was born in India shared a Western point of view
My life was prim and proper it was the English thing to do
I sought my education in medicine that's true
I found a new perception …
When my Roots I went back to …

I saw my people starving …
This was a common truth …
It became some what disarming as Spirits light shown through
My people seemed so common from a material point of view
Again it was alarming how peaceful they were too

It seemed there was no worry of things that didn't match
The food they ate they grew
As they worshiped what they'd catch
This way of life is funny from a Western Point of view
So often we're competing with our friends and colleagues too

Perhaps, if they would marry …
And make these cultures one not two?
With the help of God and love we can all be prosperous too!
Our wealth won't come from money but rather from the soul
For it's clear that when we separate it really takes its toll!

I hope that we are finding …
If by sharing what we have Universal Consciousness
Shows God's love on our behalf
Our wars they will be ending if we would only see
That just as there is one sky there is one God to set us free!

Does it really matter?

Does it really matter what happened long ago?
By using doubt for my excuses I will never ever grow
It's myself that I'm not facing by allowing fear to breed
Soon it will destroy me my judgment it will impede

I won't acknowledge good intentions
For my thoughts will be of greed
When I hide behind these demons
I make blame the common creed

Reality escapes us and my clarity does to
I must learn from my mistakes and change my point of view
For once I shift my thinking …
My past will gone too!

By discovering all new treasures …
With no limits to cut through …
Some will see me as a genius … Or a bit outlandish to
For changing thoughts and theories to different points of view

Living in the Southeast, I am all too familiar with the devastation that the hurricanes caused to businesses and personal property. However, it fails in comparison to the many lives that were lost and changed forever by the massive relocation of families. We can dwell on the downside, or we can view these relocations as blessings.

I met a woman whose family had relocated to Orlando. When I asked how her family was adjusting, she said if Katrina had not caused her family to relocate, she most likely would have lost her children to the streets, either through drugs or a drive by shooting. She explained that her eldest son, at 16, was forced to take a long, hard look at his substance addiction. He realized that he was going to have to step up to the plate and start contributing to the well being of his mother and siblings. He took the loss of their home and belongings as the cosmic 2 by 4 that hit him square between the eyes and made him realize the value of family.

While Katrina delivered a devastating blow on all it touched, for some came salvation. Even the devastated businesses and families that stayed and rebuilt were forced to revaluate the true meaning of life, and a new sense of value had to be reckoned with. It is surprising how often and how many people lose, or come close to losing, everything they have worked a lifetime for, before they wake up.

"Our individual lives cannot, generally, be works of art unless the social order is also." Charles Horton Cooley

Nowhere to Now here

I came away from *nowhere* and find myself *Now Here*
As the hardy storm blew in I lost all I thought was dear
Possessions they were ruined and families did separate
The waters flooded through what was thought a sturdy gate

We sat upon the roof tops clinging to our lives
While losing our possessions to rain and clouded skies
I thought I'd never say this but that day it was a *Blessing*
It made me see the importance of the lives that I was messing

Now it is years later and I found my family
They've all been relocated and so have I you see
Before that storm hit us you know that fateful day
I never took the time to watch the innocent children play

While now we may not have much or as much as we did before
But in retrospect I'm thinking we have Oh! So much more
Our family is together a new peace we enjoy
As we count up all our blessings and appreciate our boy!

For once he was addicted to drugs and alcohol!
But in this relocation he *"Don't do that no more"*
It was like a revelation an epiphany you see
He saw a better way of life and changed so we could be
An example for the children and a happy *fam-i- ly!*

Street War

Although I was not drafted … I went to fight my War
A personal affliction of fear and much, much, more
At the time I failed to see what my mother had become
A selfless, fearless, woman with the strength to over come
And while I was out fighting she went on with her life!
She showed me through her *strength*
To move on … despite my strife
My fears I let them guide me into a senseless haze
To manifest unhappiness from all my childhood days
I took on the mistakes of my family and my friends
Not acknowledging the pain my antics did extend
For this I will apologize for what else can I to do
I hope that with God's help I've changed this point of view
I was often self absorbed in my quest for Love and Glory
I mistook what was good guidance as just another Story
I looked at her with Judgment and a verdict I did pass
I deliberately tried to hurt her so my freedom would be cast
I denied all of the tears that lingered in my heart
I thought that with another I'd have a fresh new start!
But, it was not so easy to let my family go
My obvious confusion turned to anger as you know
I couldn't understand why they just couldn't see
I thought they understood *my* world was full of *me*
I wanted my possessions never to divide…
I didn't see the lessons…
Or comprehend the love they held inside!

George first came to see me about his troubled marriage. His wife Jeanie wanted to start a family, but he was reluctant because he felt he would not be a good father. As a child, his father was seldom home, and when he was home he was a strict disciplinarian. He was still terrorized by the mere sound of his father's voice, even though his father was well into his seventies. After several sessions of hypnosis, I regressed him back to his childhood. Almost immediately, he started to panic. Within minutes he was in a full blown anxiety attack, shaking uncontrollably, breathing in a shallow way, and he broke into a sweat.

He was displaying symptoms of hyper-arousal, which is when a mass of stress hormones flood the brain, causing feelings of confusion and befuddlement. By asking George a series of questions, I drew his attention away from the perceived threat of his father's abusive behavior. I was able to get him to refocus. I directed him to visit his safe place, which was established earlier. I moved him out of the immediate danger zone by having him witness the event as though he were a spectator. We repeated this exercise several times until he felt as though he were watching a movie, rerun after rerun. The difference was that he was able to change the outcome, because he was playing the leading role and very much in control of the script. Once he established that the threat no longer existed, he was able to release it from his subconscious mind. By repeating the scene over and over, he had desensitized his fear. He came to see his father as a frightened, insecure man who used his anger to mask his fears.

George was able to understand that if he continued to hold on to his past experiences with his father, he would bring his chamber of horrors to any children he might have in the future. Once he recognized his responsibility, he was able to release his anxiety and work through the fear.

It used to be that we could look to our elders for guidance and direction, knowing that we would hear the truth, no matter how difficult it might be to accept. Today, with all of the split families, it has become increasingly more difficult to find that safe relationship without facing judgment from a stranger, or without being compared to the *real kids* who share the same birth parents.

As I mentioned earlier in the book, our children are turning to their friends and sometimes street gangs as replacement families. Unfortunately, like attracts like, so rather than solving the problems they're making them worse, because they're being fed with misguided ignorance. Even families that manage to stay together are so stressed with finances that working overtime steals the precious bonding experiences that used to be expected as normal. It is now common for both parents to actively be in the work force. If we're to break the gender barrier, it is vital that both parents share the household duties as well. This will give an example of balance to the children and make a step forward in stopping the double standard households of yesteryear.

"Because things are the way they are, things will not stay the way they are." Bertolt Brecht

Chair of Honor

There is a Chair of Honor that's being held for you
Your hard work and persistence have paid off well it's true
Some may not recognize the sacrifice you made
They see you as one hardened so you could make the grade

Perhaps there is some truth in there point of view
So here will be your real test it will change your life for you
You've achieved your great successes and paid an awesome price
Sometimes you were just ruthless and really not so nice

Well here's another level it might be hard for you
It's a height you've never climbed it's another point of view!
Now dig into your pocket and pull out all the lint
It's like looking at your soul are you getting a small hint?

There is no corporation no board of directors too
You're on your own on this one it's clearly up to you!
Show that part of tenderness that you never before revealed
Feel that part of freedom so hidden and concealed!

I welcome you to my world of dishes, pots and pans
And then right after dinner its bath time and fairy lands
I know this may seem foreign to one the likes of you
Remember the first contract the one I made with you

We both now need to focus it's important what we do
For now we have a family and they surely need us too
You said some things to me and I said things to you
Some of them were hurtful and some of them were true

Regardless of their meaning or even the content
We must go inside our hearts to find the real intent
Relationships are painful despite what some may say
And if we want real happiness honesty is the only way

Chest Pains

I feel a major heartbreak sitting on my chest
Some thought it might be illness
I'm sure I'm just depressed I feel such disappointment
For things are out of hand I watch our families loosing it
As though the devil were in command!
Where is the dinner table? That place we used to meet
We sat around discussing things like politics and smelly feet
We got on to the fast track and lost all our good sense
Our families lost importance as we became more tense
We need to look for answers and find what was once held dear
And put into perspective what we should and should not fear
Some lives they have no focus and things won't resonate
Perhaps it's time to look around and *Re-evaluate!*

Now this may seem quite foolish … but it's become real clear
If we don't change our patterns and cease defending what we hear
Our families will be dinosaurs facing icebergs with great fear
With our extinction viewed as etchings on a subway wall
Gangs will raise our children and they will never know
Loyalty and family will be like a Broadway show
We must set our boundaries or pay the consequence
Stop acting as defeated and get our asses off the fence!
Have vibrations been so thickened …
And we've become so dense …
That we forgot God sent us angels
Perhaps it's time to now commence
We will open up our hearts …
And feed our minds with *Common Sense!*

Grieving

I know life is an *Illusion* and grief is a *Fantasy*
It creeps into my soul and possesses a part of me
You stayed here for a while you made this place your home
And as I look around I sit here all alone

Your things are here and there and I see that you're nowhere
But I feel your soul around me surrounding me with care
The love that you once gave me you openly would share
It didn't matter who it was your kisses were always there

You left me here in tears I'm really missing you
But, I know that this *Illusion* will come right back to you
I'm probably real selfish to carry on this way
But, you were my *"Warm Fuzzy"* through out each given day

Deep down inside my heart I know that this is true
That we will meet again and I will know it's you
Your eyes will start to twinkle as we come into view
And I will know the feeling of always *Loving you!*

Little Birdie

There was a little birdie that came to me last night
She whispered in my ear with concern and a bit of fright
She said, that you're still hurting from the loss of a great love
And your actions have been foolish and not guided from above
I know your pain is real and resentment has set in
But ask yourself this question …
Why are you allowing him to win?

Life is what it is and that you cannot change
Don't rent out your good spaces …
Perhaps, it's time to re-arrange …
Your gifts they are many so count them one by one
You'll see that you are bountiful despite this son of a gun
Ask yourself this question is what you're thinking really true?
And what would your life be like if it turned around for you?

You can do this Darlin, the choice is yours at last
You can drown yourself in misery … Or put away your past
You'll find once you release it a peace worth more then gold
So stop this foolish party before it makes you old
Choose to look within for that is where you'll find
Spirit waits to mend your soul … And give you peace of mind!

Max and Stephanie were twins who were raised in a highly competitive, athletic family. Max felt that he was under constant scrutiny to compete and win in the sport of the season. When he tried to tell his overbearing, jock father that he was interested in theater, his words would fall on deaf ears, or they were rebuffed by comments like, "Theater is for sissies. Real men don't read Shakespeare. That's not even freaking English."

Stephanie, on the other hand, really excelled in softball and tennis. She wanted to pursue a career in coaching, but her father would not hear of it. And when she would attempt to share her goals with her father, his comment was, "You're just a girl, how would you know anything about sports?"

Her dad was obviously failing to accept that the X/O chromosomes in his children were reversed. Stephanie had masculine tendencies, and Max was more feminine. Their dad was denying the obvious, and his homophobic fears were controlling him. While he loved both of the twins, he was unable to deal with the humiliation of their sexual differences. As a result, the twins were forced to take on exterior personas that were totally foreign to their true selves.

As parents, friends, and teachers, we so often fail to really listen, not even honoring the feelings of another. By not doing so, we force our views on them and then take offense when our ideas are rejected, or we feel that our opinions are the only ones that count and if things are not handled the way we think they should be, then the whole world is going to hell in a hand basket. If the person seeking the advice, or just asking to be heard, is not of strong mind, they are bulldozed into someone else's world, sometimes finding that years later the advice was not really needed, only a sympathetic ear.

Most people seeking a good listener choose a family member or friend who is more interested in serving their own agenda or solving your problem, rather than allowing you to vent so you can find your own answers. Our ego takes great pride in having all the answers. Another scenario is one of not wanting the other person to enjoy their success, because our lives may pale in comparison.

A selfless person will feel immeasurable pride when acknowledging the success of another. A jealous person will wallow in envy and resentment, while wasting their own opportunities and talents, either because they are insecure with themselves or just plain lazy. When encountering this negativity, it would be wise to walk away, or if the person is someone you love, thank them for sharing and take their criticism as a constructive tool to spur you on to achieve your personal goal. By changing your thought process, you can find great strength in adversity.

"It is the mark of an educated mind to be able to entertain a thought without accepting it." Aristotle

Fields of happiness

Just to say I love you
Would never be enough
I hold you in a special place
Like a diamond in the rough
Like fields of wheat
I've watched you sow
You were always such an optimist
Full of life and a loving glow

Your obstacles were challenges
From which you've always rose above
You gave out your forgiveness
With unconditional love
I see you as a leader
A teacher of great peace
You will guide so many others
To forgive and then release

Your innocence shows wisdom
Through truth and purity
I pray it won't be tainted
By immaturity
Remember to seek guidance
From his Holiness above
By surrounding yourself with the light
Of Gods, unconditional love

Believe

There are no distant heights that you can not explore
By believing in yourself you will find them and many more!
Set your goals so high that you'll look them in the eye
Know that believing in *yourself* is like taking candy off a shelf

And, if there is a time that you may have some doubt?
Go straight into your heart and let your Spirit out
Let Spirit be your guide for it will set you Free
And lead you down the path to Peace and Harmony!

When life is not so easy and it does not seem so fair
See, it as a *Challenge* one that you will dare!
Your strength is in your Soul and it will shine right through
I know you have the Wisdom its deep inside of you!

I feel that I can say this and I know that it is true
I see your wisdom growing and your *"Loving Kindness"* too
When many years have past and I am gone from you
Remember that I love you and *"I Believe in you"!*

Good or Bad

There is no good or bad life is just what it is
Our punishment and judgment limit where we live
By forgiving all our trespassers from sins deep in our pasts
We'll find with truth a happiness that change will surely last

By allowing all our worries to control what we can't view
We manifest the limits and fail to see what we can do
So cast aside you doubts and focus on your dreams
They'll be delivered by your efforts arriving on moonbeams

Some say to let God do it but what they do not see
Is if we don't put forth an effort our souls will not be free
God's the perfect parent he'll make us account for our mistakes
To take our lives for granted will close the pearly gates

We will have to start all over same lessons different names
Our freewill and our choices provide solutions to old games
So drop this selfish armor and tell yourself the truth
For you may lie to many others but you can never lie to you

Century after century, our cultures have suffered from war, either to acquire new territories, conquer civilizations, or master the seas. Our most compelling reasons were to defend our deities, or God, in massive attempts to make our world, your world. One would think that after thousands of years of apparent failures, we would realize there is no right way, nor is there a wrong way. There is just "The Way," which is one of accepting life for its challenges, its defeats, and its victories, then to take complete ownership of what we have created for ourselves.

Confucius says, "In the archer there is a resemblance to the mature person. When he misses the mark, he turns and seeks the reason for his failure in himself."

The Tao

I once had a religion with fear and so much blame
I was afraid… to voice my opinion
Or take possession… of my shame
So I decided to go further
I researched my thoughts and doubts

I found an … Ancient philosophy
That could straightened nations out
The Tao… it's not a scripture
Nor a religious … point of view
It is a way of life

That when paid attention to
It teaches acceptance of us the way we are
So that we won't pass judgment
And punish like a Czar
It is something we won't label

Just something we… will do
Once we see the God in us
This Source will guide us through
Our lives become so peaceful
That *Wars* we will not view

Time

There is a time for *Sorrow*
And a time for *Peacefulness*

There is a time for *Knowledge*
And then for *Ignorance*

There is a time *Love*
And a time for *Hatred* too

We must complete this circle
It is our lot in life to do

Remember… who you are
Is all you really have

So let go of your Ego
And show your better half!

Life is one grand presentation of challenges and consequences, memories and coming attractions. It has always been fascinating to me to observe and share my inner most thoughts and perceptions of myself and those around me. You may find as I did, that when observing these actions, we acquire an ability to reveal and sometimes understand why we do the things we do. I trust that you will find that part of you silently waiting to recognize your perfection. No matter what you may be experiencing, it is exactly as it should be. Once you accept this, you will allow yourself to attract and manifest your hearts desire.

Start by loving yourself.

"You cannot be lonely if you like the person you're alone with"
Dr. Wayne Dyer

Our Anchor

Our anchor to the Universe
Is our unconditional love

It is something we've been gifted
By Spirit from above

It is a lesson if we choose it
To share and give out free

We'll experience eternal peace
When we are the best that we can be

About the Author

Diane lives in Central Florida with her husband, Richard, and her pets: Heidi, a Rottweiler, Bambi, a Chihuahua, and her Calico cat, Gabby. She has two children, five step children, and eleven grandchildren. In 2000, she and her husband opened Alternate Pathways Inc., a Holistic Information Center, where she conducts workshops for stress and anger management. She is a Certified Hypnotist, a NLP Practitioner, a Minister for the Alliance of Divine Love, and she has a BA and a Master's Degree in Conflict Resolution. In her spare time she is a volunteer at the "Anthony House," a homeless shelter in Zellwood, Florida. She encourages her clients to de-stress through meditation, self hypnosis and various other workshops. Her poetry is an expression of her observations and real life experiences. It is her intention to touch a special place in the heart of every reader and open a personal window to reality.

"For generations man has hidden behind his fears and vulnerabilities by displaying random acts of disrespect and violence. It is my belief that if we expose these weaknesses in a safe, creative setting, they will become workable. Our dysfunctional families will come out of the shadows, and our Souls will be free to express and accept life just as it is with its perfect imperfections".

"The Gathering", audio book will be available in the spring of 2008 it can be purchased through the web site: www.alternatepathways.com. For more information or to book speaking engagements, Diane can be contacted through her e-mail address: diane@alternatepathways.com.